21 DAY
PR
ACTION GUIDE

THE WHO, WHAT, WHEN AND WHERE
TO LAUNCH A SUCCESSFUL PR CAMPAIGN

DREW GERBER + MICHELLE TENNANT

Wasabi Publicity, Inc.
438-B Highway 176 East
Saluda, NC 28773-8686

Published in the United States by The Art of Aha! Publishing,
a division of Wasabi Publicity, Inc., Saluda, North Carolina.

ISBN: 978-0-9894575-4-5

Printed in the United States of America

21 Day PR Action Guide

Table of Contents

WEEK ONE – Creating Your Secret Weapon:
Your Online Press Kit

Let's start with the basics: A press kit is **not** your website!

A press kit is *specifically designed* to *serve the media's needs*. It has *specific components* within a *particular organization*.

Think of a recipe: A well-organized, concise recipe is easy to follow. But a recipe that is jumbled and unclear, full of extraneous material and wandering explanation? A cook's worst nightmare!

It isn't hard to put a good press kit together. You already have almost everything you need. You'll just need to tweak your materials so they support you in a vibrant and successful PR campaign.

Basic ingredients

About You: This is copy that talks about your purpose or mission, service or product or invention.

You'll tweak it on Day 3 to feature the unique or the poignant, the "how it solves our problems" and "why we should care" aspects of what you've got.

Your Bio: Who you are and what's your experience.

On Day 4, you'll create versions that work for radio, print, investigative and more in-depth media.

Media Coverage: Clips or articles that have featured. you.

If you've got some good ones, great! If not, you'll build this as you get more coverage.

News and Story Ideas: Interesting angles that the media might use to feature you.

On Day 6, you'll create some evergreen like health, sex, money and relationships, as well as other topics that are seasonal or specific to current trends.

Questions & Answers:
A variety of questions you want to be asked that will entertain, enlighten, or educate the audience.

You'll create these questions and some good answers on Day 7.

That's pretty much it. Commit 30 minutes per day and follow the outlined steps, and **by the end of this week, you'll have a complete press kit.**

But before you even begin your press kit, it's important to know why the heck you're even doing PR at all!

DAY 1 – The Why of It All:
What Do You Want From Public Relations?

We can show you how to create a killer press kit (and we will over the next few days) or how to write the perfect pitch (next week, we promise) or how to become a Media Darling with all kinds of shows vying to have you on their dance card (yep, that's coming too!)

But if you don't know *why* you're doing PR and what you hope to gain from it, well, the rest is just stuff and nonsense.

So let's use this first day to give you a Primer on why PR can be so effective in getting you what you want. Then figure what it is you *do* want.

1. To Market, To Market

Every great marketing plan has *three legs*:

Sales is when someone talks to you directly, trying to persuade you to buy their product or service.

Advertising is that paid ad or commercial that someone created to try to convince you to buy what they've got.

But *PR* is more like hearing your best friend rave about something awesome, piquing your interest.

As adults, we've seen behind the marketing curtain and we're all pretty cynical about those first two legs. We also don't like to be manipulated, so most of us push against "being sold." But with public relations, we don't feel that squishy pressure of someone trying to get us to do something. Instead, we're intrigued, attracted, eager. And *that* makes PR powerful.

2. Street Cred

Imagine this: You hear some guy standing in front of you in the line at Starbucks, spouting his theory about the origin of the universe. Eh. Now imagine seeing that same guy on *Fox News* or *Dr. Oz* or sitting across from Bill Nye and Neil deGrasse Tyson on *Cosmos*. Has your perspective shifted? You betcha! Simply because **that guy is on TV or radio or in print, we assume he knows** (or at least, that *somebody important* thinks he knows) what he's talking about. Instantly, **that guy has more credibility**. And so will you.

3. Heard It Through the Grapevine

You can personally tell your story or promote your cause to *hundreds* of individuals. You can send *thousands* of emails or postcards. You can pay up the nose for regional or even national ads. But the megaphone of the media can get your message out to *zillions of people in a nanosecond*. **PR acts like a virus** that is highly contagious. (And I mean this in the most positive way!) One media outlet runs your story then a different outlet picks it up, then another and another until it reaches audiences you didn't even know existed—audiences who nevertheless are interested in *You!*

4. Up Close and Personal

We all prefer to do business and get involved with people we like and trust, right? Typically, **good PR helps people connect to you** as someone they can like and trust. They may not meet you personally, but when they see you on TV or hear you on the radio or read your articles and blogs, they begin to feel they know you. And by knowing you, they feel connected to your product, service, or cause.

5. Giving to Get

Unlike sales and advertising, in a PR campaign you spend very little time *asking* people to buy, donate, or sign-up. Most of your time is spent in **giving your knowledge**, your insights, and your expertise. When you give folks something of value, the appreciation they feel often translates into giving *you* what you want—with very little asking on your part!

6. Unexpected Doors Opening

Because PR focuses on you, your expertise and insights, it often **opens unexpected doors** that sales and advertising don't. For example, an ad that extolls the brilliance of your latest book might sell that book. But a PR campaign that reveals how brilliant, witty, well-informed and personable *you* are may lead to speaking engagements, consulting gigs, and other business opportunities *as well as* selling that book!

7. Know What You Want

Because PR can offer such a smorgasbord of benefits, it's important to figure out exactly what *you* want from it. Otherwise, you'll be wandering around the buffet table, picking at foods you don't really like and never feeling full! Do you wish to **become a household name** in a specific area of expertise? Are you looking to **promote a certain event** or cause, or sell **a particular product**? And if so, what kinds of results would signal success to you? Once you get some of that limelight, what specific outcomes do you intend to produce with it?

Day One Action Steps

The following questions will help you get clear about where you're currently at and your goals for your PR campaign. Do NOT start rubbing that bottle to let the PR genie out until you have this clarity!

1. **What are your current revenues? What would you like them to be in 6 months? One year? Five years?**

2. **Why did you begin your career/passion/organization? What is most important about it now?**

3. **What websites and blogs do you currently have? How well and in what ways are they working for you?**

_____

_____

_____

_____

_____

_____

_____

4. **What other marketing vehicles have you used (sales, ads, etc.)? How well and in what ways are they working for you?**

_____

_____

_____

_____

_____

_____

_____

5. **What kind of social media have you used? How do you use it? How well does social media work for you?**

_____

_____

_____

_____

_____

_____

_____

6. **What products or services do you offer? Of those, which are most important to promote now? Why?**

_____

_____

_____

_____

_____

_____

_____

7. **What new products or services would you like to offer? When would you like to start offering them?**

_____

_____

_____

_____

_____

_____

8. **Who are your current clients or customers? Who would you like to attract in the future?**

_____

_____

_____

_____

_____

9. **How large would you like your client/customer base to be in six months? One year? Five years?**

_____

_____

_____

_____

_____

10. Complete the following statements:

From a ***revenue perspective***, my goal for this PR campaign is to generate $_____

by _____ (date).

From a ***career perspective***, my goal for this PR campaign is to

_____

_____

_____

_____

(i.e. clients, expansion of offerings, new opportunities, etc.)

by _____ (date)

From a ***personal perspective***, my goal for this PR campaign is to

_____

_____

_____

(i.e. skills you'd like to enhance, particular accomplishments that would be satisfying, etc.)

by _____ (date)

My other specific goals for this PR campaign include:

_____ by _____ (date)

_____ by _____ (date)

_____ by _____ (date)

DAY 2 – Meet Your New Best Friend: What the Media Really Wants

Let me introduce you to the person who's going to help you get all the good things you want from PR, your new best friend, Ms. Media. Ms. Media comes in all shapes and sizes—radio, TV, internet, or print. She's male, female, young and not-so-young, all ethnicities. She's local, national, even international.

But no matter who Ms. Media is at any given moment, she's got several things in common:

1. She's in a hurry! It's either *right now* or *never*.

Ms. Media needs what she needs *now*, not tomorrow or next week or next month when you get your act together. So before you introduce yourself, be prepared to give her what she needs *now*.

2. She's on a *mission*: to Entertain, Enlighten, and Educate.

That is her job. That is her passion. That is the reason she exists. If she doesn't consistently entertain, enlighten, and educate her audience, she's toast. So she needs *a constant flow of good material* to survive.

3. She doesn't give a damn about you unless you can help her do #2.

You might be a superb person. But if you can't contribute to her *constant flow of good material* to *entertain, enlighten, and educate her audience,* her very survival *demands* that she ignore you. (Nothing personal.)

4. She will *adore* you if you can *really* help her do #2.

She is constantly bombarded by people who don't know what she needs and have nothing to offer to help her *entertain, enlighten,* and *educate* her audience. If you are one of the few who really can give her what she needs, that's OMG! Best Friends Forever!

5. She doesn't have nearly enough time to meet all her deadlines.

It's all 24/7. Her audience is voracious. The next story is due before the last one has aired or gone to print. She has to think months in advance then grab that last minute lead before anybody else does.

6. Thou shalt not waste her time!

She's working an impossible schedule. So feeding her material that doesn't fit her needs, spinning her wheels by making her chase down photos or clips, sucking up her precious minutes with idle chit chat—it's just *plain cruel*. And she won't forget it.

7. She will adore you if you make things easier and faster for her.

Ah, but if you are the one in a million who gets right to the point, has all your material in a convenient place, refers her to other great resources if you aren't a good fit—she'll name her firstborn after you.

8. She's a real-live human person. Treat her as such. Be thoughtful.

99 out of 100 people simply want to use her. They don't acknowledge that great article she just published or that fascinating interview she produced. They don't notice that she just ran her first marathon or got promoted. If she's going to be your new best friend, shouldn't you pay attention to those things?

9. You are here to serve her and her mission, *not* the other way around.

Yep, it's all about her and her voracious audience. It's all about making it easy and even fun for her. And, yes, I know you have an amazing charity in Africa or a spectacular invention or a brilliant book—but this relationship is all about how you can fulfill *her* needs.

10.   By honoring #9, you *will* get all you need.

And this is the golden key that so many people miss: If you provide Ms. Media all that she needs, she will be incredibly, almost frighteningly, generous.

BEST FRIENDS FOREVER

This new best friend might sound pretty high maintenance. But once you understand her and work with her on her terms, she's really delightful to be with. And she can open up opportunities for you that you *never* even imagined!

And because she is so vital to your success, you're going to create a site that is for *Her Use Only*.

YOUR PRESS KIT

To break it down, just keep *two main themes* in mind when approaching Ms. Media:

#1 Time: Don't waste it. Help her save it. Be brief and to the point.

#2 It's ALL About Her Mission: ENTERTAIN, ENLIGHTEN, and EDUCATE.

Give her what she needs. ALWAYS fit into one, if not all three, of those categories for her.

Day Two Action Steps

Let's start turning your thinking inside out. To paraphrase John F. Kennedy, "Ask not what the media can do for you. Ask what *you* can do for the media." How can you help Ms. Media to...?

1. **ENTERTAIN: Brainstorm and list as many ways as you can think of that you could help entertain her audience**. Can you share great stories? Do you have a humorous perspective on events? Can you juggle while analyzing the stock market? Pay attention to ways others who appear in the media are entertaining to you.

_____

_____

_____

_____

2. **ENLIGHTEN: What insights or wisdom do you have to share?** What fresh perspectives can you bring to old topics? What new questions can you raise that will benefit her audience?

_____

_____

_____

_____

3. **EDUCATE: What can you teach people that will help solve their problems?** What practical knowledge do you have that a typical person doesn't? What resources can you tell them about that would help them get where they want to go?

_____

_____

_____

_____

4. **ENLIST** a colleague, friend, or spouse to help you brainstorm these same questions. Ask this person, "How do you think I can Entertain, Enlighten and/or Educate the media's audience?"

_____

_____

_____

_____

_____

_____

_____

_____

_____

_____

_____

_____

DAY 3 – Standing Out from the Crowd: Quirks at Work

So you've got tons of experience in your chosen profession and degrees up the wazoo. You can explain your product or service in detail to even the most sophisticated listener and field impossible questions. Your IQ is off the charts and you have incredible gifts and talents to share.

And no one cares

Well, they do care a little. But all those degrees and experience and knowledge do *not* make you warm and fuzzy. They don't make you relatable and frankly, they don't make you unique and interesting. And if you aren't interesting to Ms. Media's audience, you aren't interesting to her.

However, you *do* have things about you that *are* interesting and *will* grab Ms. Media's attention. Some of them relate directly to what you're promoting and some may not:

1. Your Story

Everybody loves a good story. Your childhood, your history, where you grew up (Ms. Media loves to cover hometown heroes). How you got from A to Z. Your birthdate (do you match Ms. Media's target audience demographic?).

2. Your Challenges

It's hard to relate to people who have had no challenges in life. We root for the underdog or the guy who blows it then finds a way to redeem himself. But a person who has made no mistakes? Who's had smooth sailing and everything handed to him on a silver platter? BORING!

3. Your Motivation

We love to understand what drives people to do what they do. Whether it's a childhood incident or an Aha moment, we are fascinated by what drives them forward. We want to know what keeps you going when the going gets rough.

4. Your Passions

Nothing is more exciting than a person who is passionate! Even if we are in direct opposition to whatever someone is passionate about, aren't we intrigued by the passion itself? So is Ms. Media. Not just about your passion for your work or business, but *all* of your passions.

5. Your Quirks

Is there really such a thing as "normal?" We all have dumb little things we do or silly rituals or irritating habits we won't give up. It's what makes us human—and in a way, endearing.

6. Your Unique Insights or Perspectives

We all view life through lenses that have been colored by our experiences and beliefs. Think about your viewpoint on specific topics or the world in general. How does it differ from the crowd?

7. Your Winning Edge

Your winning edge is about comparing yourself to your competition or others in your field. It's the ways that you are different and/or better. It's about the specific clientele that you are uniquely qualified to serve. It's about your particular approach or the results you alone can produce.

8. Your Hobbies

Think about Rosie Grier, the 6'5" former defensive lineman in the AFL, who does needlepoint in his spare time. Or Johnny Depp, who plays Barbies with his daughter. Claudia Schiffer collects insects and David Arquette knits. Don't their hobbies make them a bit more relatable, attractive, and interesting?

9. Your Secrets

Everybody loves secrets! Nothing makes us feel closer to someone than when they let us in on a secret. It doesn't have to be a big, deep, dark, scandalous secret. But isn't it interesting that Beyoncé (who has launched several perfumes) is allergic to perfume? Or that Nicole Kidman is afraid of butterflies? But be smart, and don't give Ms. Media an embarrassing secret.

Does this feel like baring your soul and going to confessional? In a way it is.

The key is that the more vulnerable and real you are, the more interesting and attractive you become.

Day Three Action Steps

The following exercises will help you dig into what is *unique and interesting* about you and your business. As you tweak your existing materials for your press kits, you'll start incorporating these *unique and interesting* elements to get Ms. Media's attention.

Because it's hard to see ourselves and our unique attributes clearly, enlist friends, colleagues or family to help you.

1. Your Story

Jot down everything: When you were born, where you grew up and went to school, what kind of childhood you had. How did you choose your career? Are you married or single? Do you have kids? Give us a brief history of your life.

_____

_____

_____

_____

_____

_____

_____

_____

_____

_____

_____

_____

_____

2. **Your Challenges**

What internal or external dragons have you faced? What daunting mountains have you had to climb? What impossible brick walls have you had to climb over, dig under or blast through? What has broken your heart?

_____

_____

_____

_____

_____

_____

_____

_____

3. **Your Motivation**

What keeps you up at night? What pulls you out of bed in the morning? What is the driving force, the fire in your belly that keeps you doing what you do?

_____

_____

_____

_____

_____

_____

_____

_____

4. Your Passions

What do you adore? What completely engrosses you so that you lose all track of time? What would you pursue even if you didn't get paid for it?

_____

_____

_____

_____

_____

_____

_____

_____

5. Your Quirks

What makes you a little odd or different? What are your eccentricities? What about you makes people laugh or roll their eyes or do a double take?

_____

_____

_____

_____

_____

_____

_____

_____

6. Your Unique Insights or Perspectives

How do you see the world, particular events, or other people a bit differently than the crowd? Do you have a novel take on a particular topic?

_____

_____

_____

_____

_____

_____

_____

_____

7. Your Winning Edge

How are you different and/or better than your competition or others in your field? What specific markets do you serve? How are the results you produce different or better? What have clients or customers complimented you on?

_____

_____

_____

_____

_____

_____

_____

_____

8. **Your Hobbies**

What activities do you enjoy? What do you find engrossing, where time seems to fly by? What fascinates you?

_____

_____

_____

_____

_____

_____

_____

_____

9. **Your Secrets**

What are some surprising things about you? Things that most people, maybe even your close friends, don't know?

_____

_____

_____

_____

_____

_____

_____

_____

DAY 4 – The Critical First Impression: Your Press Kit Home Page

Let's just refresh your memory about your new BFF, Ms. Media:

- **She's in a *hurry*** and
- **All she cares about is *entertaining, enlightening, and educating* her audience.**

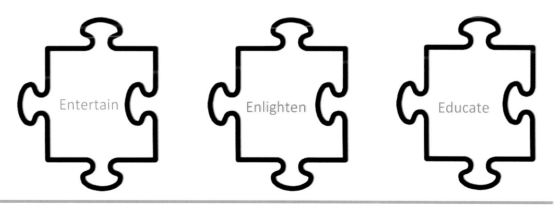

Everything in your press kit, starting with your Home Page, *must* take those two things into consideration. If not, you're just using your new secret weapon to shoot yourself in the foot.

But here's how you can create a press kit to snag Ms. Media instead.

1. Create a Headline

Catchy, bold, memorable, intriguing. This is often (though not always) **about them, not you**. ("Experience Immediate Healing!" vs. "Amazing Healer Hits Town!") Like headlines on magazine covers, it should grab Ms. Media's attention and make her crave more.

2. Write a Tagline

A short, maybe **thought-provoking phrase** that's more specific to your particular shtick. For example, "Combining ancient practices with modern psychology to overcome chronic fatigue" or "Providing a Faith-based Approach to Physical Fitness."

3. Keep It BRIEF

Be concise! The ENTIRE Home Page should be **no more than 750 words**. Do **not explain** the **obvious**. Do **not go** into **detail**. Omit flowery, empty adjectives and adverbs. If the sentence or paragraph still makes sense without a certain word or phrase, slash it out.

4. Use Short Paragraphs

- *First* paragraph: Juicy problems people have and how you solve them.
- *Second* paragraph: Brief credentials. Why should people listen to *you*?
- *Remaining* paragraphs: Explain your product or service in slightly more depth. State benefits people have received.

5. Don't Hide Gems in the Mud

Figure out your **3 or 4 main points**, and hit them hard. Don't stuff your main points or catchiest phrases in the middle of lengthy paragraphs. Set them off by themselves, make them bold or italicized. Busy people will *skim*, they don't *read*.

6. Use Plain English

Unless your target market is sophisticated professionals within your own industry, and trade or academic journals, **don't use fancy industry jargon**. Don't use $100 words when a 50 cent word will do. Be conversational and personal, not scholarly, and abstract—*unless* that's who you're trying to attract.

7. Have Personality

If you're a humorist, be funny. If you're a therapist, sound understanding, and calm. If you're a business turn-around expert, express decisiveness and confidence. Whoever you are, sound like you.

8. Use Third Person

Most of your press kit should be written as if someone else (like a journalist or publicist, not your mother) is writing it about you and your work. The nifty trick here is that you can **intersperse "quotes" from yourself** to break up the copy, make a specific point and add interest.

9. E, E, & E

What you say on this page must entertain, enlighten, and/or educate Ms. Media. It should make her laugh or cry or captivate her. It should give her hope or open up her world view. It should offer solutions to her problems. It should teach her or her audience something *useful* that she didn't know.

10. Clear links to further info

Do not make her guess where to go for further information! If you've caught her attention, typically she'll want to know more about you, what kinds of topics you can speak to, more detail about your product or service, where else in the media you've appeared, photos of you, your regular website.

Make links to these things **OBVIOUS**.

11. Clear Contact Information

You've worked hard to get Ms. Media salivating so don't leave her hanging! Make your contact information clear *and* make sure when she uses it, she gets an immediate response. If you're often unavailable, an assistant or marketing person might be a better contact. If it's best to reach you at certain times, let Ms. Media know. (Just keep in mind that Ms. Media does not have time to fit *your* finicky schedule within *her* frantic schedule.)

Day Four Action Steps

Let's build your Home Page *step-by-step*. You'll be able to pull in material you already have. But remember *who* we're creating this for and tweak accordingly!

By the way, the only way you'll get through these actions steps in 30 minutes is if you don't over-think it. Just write, don't edit. You can clean it up and spruce it up later.

And if you're not quite sure about any aspects of your Home Page, no worries! In the Appendix at the end of this book, you'll find several excellent examples to guide you.

1. Your 3 to 4 Main Points

What are the *3 or 4 critical things* Ms. Media needs to know about you or your work? (And, no, you can't expand it to 5 or 6 points.) If those main points aren't obvious, begin with 10 points. Next ask yourself, "If I could only have 9, which would I choose?" Keep eliminating until you have your 3 to 4 absolutely critical points. You'll incorporate these in your Home Page.

_____

_____

_____

_____

_____

_____

_____

_____

_____

_____

_____

2. Write Paragraph #1: Problem/Solution

What problems do people have that you can solve? Start by listing a bunch of them, preferably problems that relate to your 3 to 4 main points. Which strike you as particularly juicy, i.e. the ones that keep people up at night?

_____

_____

_____

_____

_____

_____

_____

Next to those juicy ones, write how you or your product can solve them. Finally, pick out the problem/solution combination that seems to be the most dramatic, gripping or unique. Now write that up in 2 to 3 sentences. Voila!

_____

_____

_____

_____

_____

_____

_____

_____

3. **Write Paragraph #2: Your Credentials**

Why should anyone listen to you or be impressed by your product? In 2 or 3 sentences, share only your most pertinent and impressive credentials (i.e. if you've got a Ph.D., we don't need to know that you also have a B.A.). If you written a book or received a relevant award, throw that in here.

_____

_____

_____

_____

_____

_____

_____

4. **Write 5 to 7 *Brief* Paragraphs**

Keep your paragraphs to 2 to 4 sentences. Give us more insight into what you do and who you are. Tell us a story. Share your 3 to 4 important points if you haven't already. (Hint: If this seems difficult, try writing a big long story first. Then pull out only the most interesting, critical parts and toss the rest.)

_____

_____

_____

_____

_____

_____

_____

5. Tell Them What To Do Next

"For further information, go to www.MyWebsite.com"

"Contact me for interviews at MyEmailAddress@xyz.com or by phone at 123-456-7890."

"Download my One Pager (or Free Report) here: www.MyStuff.com/OnePager"

_____

_____

_____

_____

6. Write a Headline

No more than 6 words—less is better. It should be a phrase that could have an exclamation point after it (though you won't use one). In other words, it should be exciting! "Lazy Girl's Path to True Love" "Hottest Games for Gen X'ers" "America's Financial Investigator." Look at headlines on magazines or Internet news sites to give you the sense of what works.

_____

_____

_____

_____

7. Write a Tagline

Again, checkout magazines and news sites to get the gist of a good tagline. A tagline tells a bit more but is still brief, not really a complete sentence. Use your name or product's name in it. Taglines for the Headlines above might be: "Suzie Q teaches busy (and lazy) women to find the man of their dreams in 21 days," "Gen X Products create entertaining apps that sharpen your brain," and "NY Times best-selling author Pamela Yellen shows how to grow and protect your nest egg."

_____

_____

_____

_____

8. Spruce it Up

Congratulations! You've got the first draft of your press kit Home page. To bring it to the next level, set it aside for a few days and see what other ideas pop up for you.

Ask for feedback from someone who knows your work and whose opinion you value. As you make changes and improvements, stay true to the basic structure and keep your Home page short, sweet, and compelling!

DAY 5 – Who the Heck Are You:
Creating Compelling Bios

Your press kit bio is *not* a resume.

Whether it's for radio or print or your longer bio, it tells **an interesting story about who you are**. It doesn't cover the boring details because, well, they're *boring*. It does include things you would *never* put on a job application because, well, they're *interesting*.

To paraphrase Alfred Hitchcock, "A good press-kit bio is life with all the dull bits cut out."

Remember those quirks and secrets, passions and challenges? That's what we weave into the story of *you*.

You'll create **3 versions** of your bio today:

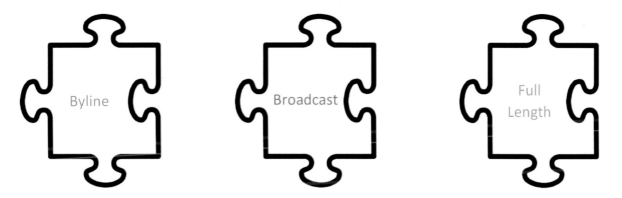

And don't panic! We've got plenty of examples to help guide you.

Your Byline (Print) Bio (under 100 words)

1. Keep It Brief

Your byline will come after an article or blog written *by* you (or sometimes *about* you). The reader was intrigued enough to want to know more about you, but the editor needs you to keep the whole byline **under 100 words**.

2. Credentials First

Lead with your most attractive credentials, the book you've written or business you've created. Start this sentence off with a phrase that describes your expertise. "Award-winning chef" or "Coach to successful entrepreneurs" or "Self-taught professional classical guitarist."

3. What You Do

What you do should be something they want! In this next sentence, **make it clear:**

- How do you help people?
- What problem does your service or product solve?

For example, "Expert college admissions coach, Jane Doe, helps clients find the best college for their children and shows them how to make it affordable."

4. How to Get More

Capitalize on the interest you've created by making it very *clear and easy* to take the next step! Most bylines today offer a **website link** or a **link to a free download** or product to draw readers in. This last sentence will simply be:

"For more information, go to www.LINK.com" or "To see how XYZ can benefit your family, download this free report at www.LINK.com/report"

Your Broadcast Bio (under 100 words)

1. It's Verbal

This is the bio a radio *interviewer will use to introduce you*. Read it out loud to make sure it flows and isn't awkward. Is your name or your product tricky to pronounce? If there is *any* doubt, show it phonetically in brackets.

For example, "Francesca Gianjorio [SAY: frahn CHESS kah   gee ahn JOR ee oh]."

2. Brief

Odds are, your interview will be 10 minutes or less. You want to use most of those minutes to intrigue listeners with your insights or solutions. Keep this radio bio *under 100 words* so it won't squander too much of your precious air time.

3. Hey, Listen to This!

The first sentence should make listeners' ears perk up. It should relate to the problems you solve and tell them specifically what they might gain from paying attention. "If you've ever been frustrated by a boss who won't acknowledge you . . ." or "For those of you who are terrified of public speaking . . ." or "Where do you turn when you run out of conventional medical options?"

4. Most Pertinent Credentials

Give your most important, pertinent credentials next. This lets the interviewer tell listeners why they should pay attention to *you* in particular on this subject.

5. Lead In

The last sentence of your radio bio can be simply, "Welcome, Dr. Kim McKean." But even better is to get the interview off to a running start: "So, Dr. McKean, you disagree with conventional wisdom when it comes to cholesterol. Why is that?" or "Dr. McKean, what is the most important thing we can do right now to lower our cholesterol?"

6. How to learn more

The interviewer should actually say this at the end of the interview. If they don't, make sure *you* do! It's simply, "To learn more, go to www.XYZ.com."

This brings up an important point: **Your website address needs to be *easy to remember*!**

(Think catchy phrase or a simple name that someone driving in rush hour traffic can quickly recall to track you down later.)

Your Full-Length Bio

This is the longer version for Ms. Media when she *really* wants to find out about you in more depth.

1. Do Everything We Said re: Your Home Page

Paragraphs should be short, *2 to 3 sentences*. Leave out extraneous words and phrases. Write in plain English, with personality, and make sure the gems don't get hidden.

2. Juicy

Your full-length bio should have interesting tidbits (quirks, passions, etc.) that Ms. Media can use to craft a story. Where you grew up, charities you support, the fact that you ran a shrink-wrap machine to get yourself through college.

3. Brief

Though extended, your long bio still can't be *long*. More than 250 words and Ms. Media will fall asleep and check out. So pick the *most interesting* of the interesting things about you.

4. Don't Start at the Beginning

Start with who you are and what you're about *today,* your expertise, accomplishments, mission, and what problems you are uniquely able to solve. In later paragraphs, you might tell the brief story of what inspired you to be who you are. You can also give a nod to your childhood if it's pertinent or interesting:

"As the child of archeologists who travelled the world. . ."

"Because he didn't learn to read until he was 12. . ."

5. Show Don't Tell

Rather than *telling* Ms. Media that you or your products are brilliant and effective, *show* her:

"Dr. Slate has successfully helped over 300 clients overcome their fear of flying."

"Sun Lighting has brought inexpensive solar energy to over 2500 families in developing countries."

"Mr. Minsk has been tapped as the keynote speaker for Toastmaster's International for 7 years running."

6. Strut Your Stuff

Bring out your *awards and accolades*. Tell them where you've been featured elsewhere in the media and how many books you've written. If you've been dubbed "the only trainer you'll ever need," say so. This is not the place to be humble.

7. Be Human

Let Ms. Media know about your family, where you live, your hobbies, your passions, your pets.

Day Five Action Steps

As you do these exercises to create your bios, keep in mind that this is the *story* of you, *not* a resume. It will include facts and figures, but only those that will get Ms. Media's attention.

1. Look at Examples

Start by looking at examples of good bios. What patterns do you see? How do they follow the guidelines above? What do you like and not like about them?

2. Edit Out the Boring Bits

Now pull up the bio you've been using for yourself, perhaps the one on your website. ***Highlight the parts that would be interesting to Ms. Media.*** These would include awards and accomplishments in your field, books you've written, places you've appeared in the media.

These would *not* include your entire educational and career history.

(Graduated from Stanford? Potentially interesting. Graduated from Podunk Junior College? Not so much. Worked for Richard Branson or Imelda Marcos? Interesting. Worked for your uncle? Probably not, unless he's Richard Branson.)

3. Rough Out a Long Bio

Following the guidelines above, use the highlighted parts to start roughing out your bio. Go back to previous days' action steps to remind yourself of passions, problems/solutions, quirks that you can weave in. Shoot for ***around 250 words***. *But do not agonize over this!* For now, a rough draft is fine.

_____

_____

_____

_____

_____

_____

_____

_____

_____

_____

_____

_____

_____

_____

_____

_____

_____

_____

_____

_____

_____

_____

_____

_____

_____

_____

_____

_____

_____

_____

_____

DAY 5 – Who the Heck Are You? Creating Compelling Bios

4. Rough Out a Broadcast Bio

Imagine an interviewer introducing you and, following the guidelines above, draft a brief (less than 100 words) radio bio. You'll be able to pull from your long bio here. **Read** your first draft **out loud**. How does it sound? Make any obvious changes. *Again, do not over-think this!* Go for a rough first draft.

_____

_____

_____

_____

_____

_____

_____

_____

_____

_____

_____

_____

_____

_____

_____

_____

_____

_____

5. Rough Out a Byline Bio

This is a condensed version (less than 100 words) from your long bio and might be similar to parts of your radio bio. Quickly draft your first version. Take a look and make obvious changes then let it alone.

_____

_____

_____

_____

_____

_____

_____

_____

_____

_____

_____

_____

_____

6. Fine Tune Them

To bring your bios to the next level, ***set them aside for a few days.*** Review the guidelines above and revisit what you've written. Ask for feedback from someone who knows your work and whose opinion you value, making sure they understand the purpose of these bios and the basic structures you need to follow.

Voila! Your bios are ready to go into your online press kit! (And keep in mind, you can always tweak them down the road!)

DAY 6 – Inspire Ms. Media:
News & Story Ideas

Ms. Media's audience is *insatiable*.

That means she is constantly hunting and scrambling for fresh, interesting stories and ideas to (c'mon now, say this with me) **entertain**, **enlighten,** and **educate**. As her new best friend, you could literally *save her career* if you can come up with fascinating stories and topics she can use—for which she will be very grateful.

And here's the key: You may not be a professional journalist or editor with an eye for great news. But you have expertise and perspective that are totally unique. You know things Ms. Media doesn't know. You've got dynamite solutions to issues and problems her audience face. You are media gold!

So on this page of your press kit, you'll give your new BFF exactly what she needs: fresh, unique story ideas. Just follow these guidelines and get inspiration from the examples in the Appendix.

1. Keep It Brief

This is a story *idea, not* the full story. Write a brief paragraph that peaks her curiosity with enough meat so she knows you can deliver. It should be 70 words or less, 2 or 3 sentences. Think of it like those story intro's newscasters deliver right before they say, "News at 11:00." ("What if you found a grizzly bear in your kitchen? With only a mop and a whistle, see how this 79-year old grandma sent a 300 lb. bear packing. News at 11:00.")

2. Focus on the Big Six: Health, Wealth, Career, Sex, Relationships, Personal Growth

Why? Because this is what we all really care about. We want to make our lives better. Sure, we'd love to eradicate world hunger, too. But on a daily basis, we're more concerned about making more money or improving our sex lives. Not all of your story ideas need to fall into these categories—but make sure some of them do.

3. Their Problems, Your Solutions

People are interested in solving their problems. And if you've got good **solutions to** those **problems**, they'll be interested in *you*. Focus on the aggravating, sleep-robbing problems you know people have. Make them *specific* (i.e. "How to Fit in that Bikini by Next Month" is much better than "How to Lose Weight"). Make sure your solution sounds unique.

4. Hot Topics and Trends

What's in the news lately? Gun control? Celebrity break-ups? The latest political scandal or Wall Street scam? Tackle topics everyone is talking about with a **fresh perspective** and unique insights.

5. Seize the Seasons

Every season has a bundle of tried and true topics to tap. Autumn? Back to school, Halloween costumes, political elections. Winter? Holiday gift giving, family gatherings, winter blues. Find a few seasonal ideas—and keep in mind, Ms. Media has to keep way ahead of the game (i.e. she begins to focus on summer vacation stories in January).

6. Juice It Up

Don't be tapioca. Be key lime pie. Forget about ketchup. Be extra-hot salsa (or at least medium-hot). Dispute the common wisdom. **Be a little controversial** or sassy. Throw down a challenge. Your story idea can't be the same old, same old ho-hum. It needs to shake her up or wake her up.

7. Grab Her Attention

Begin with a snappy headline that she can't resist. Rather than "Is the Market Improving?" try something like, "Bull Market or Just Bull?" Rather than "Is Our Educational System Failing?" how about leading with, "Are We Raising a Generation of Idiots?"

8. Give Her Variety

Come up with story ideas that range over all kinds of topics for all kinds of audiences. Ms. Media may need an idea for parents or an idea for retirees. She may need something about finding your bliss or saving up to buy your first home. You can't cover every audience and every topic but give her as much variety as you can.

9. Easy Peasy Structure

Give her an easy structure:

First: **Snappy headline** (i.e. "Risky is the New Safe" or "Tell Your Therapist to Take a Hike")

Second: **One sentence of the problem** ("If we're doing all the right things, how come we're so broke?" or "Is there a way to scratch the 7-year itch without destroying your marriage?")

Third: **One sentence of your unique solution** ("Dr. Lyons explains why lowering cholesterol is *not* the key to heart health—and reveals what is." Or "Jane Marks offers 6 tips to keep your daughter safe from sexual predators in college.")

Day Six Action Steps

It's time to build your story-idea generating muscles! Not all of the ideas you come up with in this first pass will be brilliant. No worries! You'll definitely stumble on some very usable nuggets and you'll begin to get in the rhythm of thinking this way so that story ideas flow naturally.

Give yourself a running start by reviewing the examples in the Appendix before you begin.

1. Problem/Solution Story Ideas

Pick out *at least two* of the problem/solution combinations you created on Day 3. Quickly form each one into a story idea: Write a sentence about the problem and how people suffer with it. Write a sentence about the excellent unique solution you have for it. Cap it off with a snappy headline. Done!

Combination 1

_____

_____

_____

_____

_____

_____

Combination 2

_____

_____

_____

_____

_____

_____

2. Big 6 Ideas

Pick *at least two* of the Big 6 Issues: Health, Wealth, Career, Sex, Relationships, or Personal Growth. Follow the same format: One sentence about a problem or issue within this category. One sentence about your snazzy solution. Stunning headline. Finis!

Big Idea 1

_____

_____

_____

_____

_____

_____

_____

_____

Big Idea 2

_____

_____

_____

_____

_____

_____

_____

_____

3. **Hot Topic Ideas**

What hot topics are people talking about right now? Hot topics are being blasted at you from every magazine stand, every browser home page, and every TV news show. Grab at least two of those hot topics and draft a story idea for each. One sentence about *one interesting part* of the topic everyone is talking about. One sentence about your unique perspective or solution. Catchy headline. Snap!

Hot Topic 1

_____

_____

_____

_____

_____

_____

Hot Topic 2

_____

_____

_____

_____

_____

_____

4. Seasonal Ideas

Make a list for each of the four seasons (Winter, Spring, Summer, and Autumn). What comes to mind when you think of each one? What holidays fall within them? How does the weather in each season affect us? When you have a few aspects, holidays or issues for each season, choose at least two of those thoughts and write them up as story ideas. One sentence about how that aspect, holiday or issue can be a problem for people. One sentence about your clever solution. Eye-popping headline. Voila!

Winter

_____

_____

_____

_____

_____

_____

_____

_____

Spring

_____

_____

_____

_____

_____

_____

_____

_____

Summer

_____

_____

_____

_____

_____

_____

_____

_____

Autumn

_____

_____

_____

_____

_____

_____

_____

_____

5. Spruce Them Up

Put your story ideas aside for a day or two. Come back and pick out your favorites. Enlist your trusted friend again and get feedback on which seem most compelling. These are the beginning story ideas to populate the Story and News Ideas Page of your online press kit.

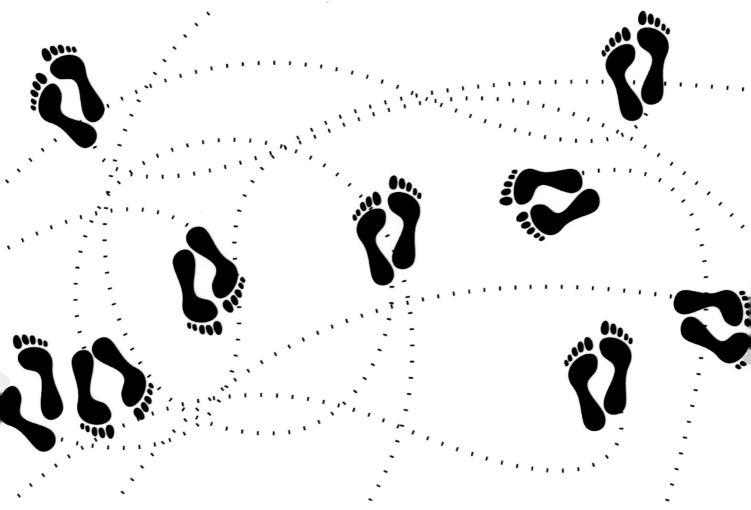

DAY 7 – Learning the Interview Dance: Interview Questions

You want to lead in the interview dance—*without* being obvious. The way you'll do this is by **feeding your interviewer irresistible questions to ask** you.

There are interviews and there are *interviews*. Though we've all watched some guest getting grilled and chopped into pieces by a snarky show host, that's fairly rare for the type of PR you're looking for—*unless* your shtick is very controversial and you are *ready, willing, and able* to bring it on!

Most of your opportunities will be venues where *the host or interviewer will look good if you look good*. Providing them fascinating questions that you can answer brilliantly is the best way for you *both* to shine.

So how do you create an irresistible interview question?

1. Do NOT Promote Yourself

What?!? Isn't that the point of all this? To promote your product or service? Yes and no—but let's focus on "no."

1) Your objective in a PR campaign is to *serve Ms. Media's needs*.

2) If you do this, Ms. Media will find opportunities to *showcase you*.

3) Her audience will *benefit* by your presence which is *very attractive* and when people are attracted to you,

4) They will automatically want whatever you have to offer. (***But you will not be successful if you try to skip 1, 2, and 3*** and go directly to #4.)

"So, why should we all run out and buy your book?" is *not* an irresistible question! But "Since you've never even attempted to write or get published before, what made you think you could do it?" just might be.

2. Be Indirect

Set yourself up **to talk about your area of expertise**, not just your product or service specifically. If you have an educational program, develop questions that relate to teachers, students, and parents. If you run a grief recovery program, talk about grief in general and ways to cope or process different losses. People need to be attracted and intrigued by *your expertise and insight* before they will care about your particular offering.

3. E, E & E

You know this by now: Your questions and your answers to those questions must entertain, enlighten, and/or educate Ms. Media's audience. You want to be so compelling or entertaining that you become what NPR calls "a garage interview"—the interview a listener can't bear to turn off, even when they've made it home and are sitting in their own garage!

4. What's In It for Them?

Even if you're revealing fascinating tidbits from your personal history, there still has to be *something* in it for the audience. How will they be changed for better from hearing this question and its answer? What new resources will they have? What new insight or inspiration? Even if it's just giving them a few chuckles during their morning commute, you must **give them something of value.**

5. Do Inquiring Minds Really Want to Know?

Yes, I know, it's terrific that your scooter has dual brakes and front-end suspension and an adjustable tiller angle—but who cares? Rather than, "What makes your scooter superior to others on the market?" how about, "If I buy a scooter for my grandma, how can I be sure she'll be safe using it?" *That's* a question someone would care about—and an answer people want to hear!

6. Ruffle Some Feathers

Bringing up a *controversial topic* or taking *an unusual stance* on something makes the audience perk up their ears. It's not about being nasty or obnoxious. It's about adding a little spice or drama.

Compare "What can parents do better to teach kids about money?" to "How are most modern parents sabotaging their kids' ability to handle money?" Or how about, "What makes your personal growth workshops so effective?" versus, "Where do you think most personal growth programs have missed the boat?"

7. Get Real, Get Personal

Theory is fine but most of us relate better to real life examples. Rather than "How does your therapy treat fear of flying?" try something like, "Can you tell us about a particularly difficult case of fear of flying that you worked with?" Using your own stories works too. Try "How has this discovery changed your life personally?" rather than "What is important about this discovery?"

8. Change It Up

Good interviewers know their audience and what their audience responds to. When developing your Interview Questions Page, make sure you have a smorgasbord of various types of questions.

9. Have Awesome Answers Ready!

The most fascination questions in the world won't do much good if you can't answer them or if your answers are just ho-hum. Make sure you have responses ready that are as

Juicy,

Delightful,

Entertaining,

Enlightening, and

Educational as the questions themselves!

Day Seven Action Steps

To take the lead in this interview dance, let's develop those irresistible questions. Begin by reviewing the great examples in the Appendix. Pay attention to which questions interest you and which bore you. Which would make you perk up your ears to hear the response?

1. Ask a Zillion Questions

Just brainstorm. Think of every question—from the brilliant to the ridiculous—that someone could ask you. What great questions have you been posed in the past about what you do? What do people ask most frequently about your work? What is the burning question you'd *love* someone to ask? Write as many as you can as quickly as you can.

_____

_____

_____

_____

_____

2. Find Your Sweet Spots

Which of these questions can you *answer brilliantly*? Which showcase your expertise or your humor or your insight? Which of these questions can you answer better than anyone else? Highlight the particular questions that will help you shine.

_____

_____

_____

_____

3. Are They Irresistible?

Judging by the 9 guidelines above, which of your questions really fit the bill? Enlist your trusted buddy again and get feedback.

WEEK TWO – Bait the Line:
Your Pitch

Just like baseball, all the action begins with a pitch.

You've prepared a great online press kit and developed interesting ways to present your valuable information. You've created a bio that sparkles and have one-pagers that give a great snapshot of who you are and how entertaining, educational, and enlightening you can be.

But so far, it's like singing in the shower: You may have a voice that rivals Josh Groban or Adele, but ain't no recording contract coming until someone besides your cat hears you!

The action (your PR campaign) doesn't start until you purposely draw attention—specifically, Ms. Media's attention—to yourself and what you have to offer via your pitch.

The pitching part of your PR campaign has several parts but it isn't complicated. Basically, it boils down to:

1) **Generate** an attractive idea for a story or how you can contribute to an existing story,

2) **Present** your ideas, usually through email, to people who could use them to educate, entertain or enlighten their audiences, and

3) **Follow-up** to gauge how interested they are in what you've presented.

That's it.

The rules for pitching are not set in stone. That said, the guidelines you'll learn in this week have proven to be *highly effective*. I suggest you adhere to them closely. Later when you have some experience under your belt, you can experiment with bending these guidelines.

DAY 8 – Who You Gonna Call?
Your Perfect Media Match

It's just like the wonderful world of dating: You can't just pursue everyone on the planet who happens to be single and the right gender. If you're looking for that perfect someone, you gotta narrow the field down first.

And when the field is a bit more manageable, (say, guys who love to travel or gals who can make you laugh) you need to come up with the approach that will catch their interest so you can explore whether you two are a match.

1. Even a Shotgun Must Be Aimed

It's true that you'll be pursuing more than one Ms. Media at a time. But unless you've decided to devote all of your waking and some of your should-be-sleeping hours to your PR efforts, you need to make sure you spend what time you have *wisely*. That means focusing on media that serves your target market.

2. Everybody or Certain Bodies?

Okay, so a kazillion people tune into The Today Show and zillions read *O Magazine* every month. You very well may get to the point where Ellen wants to interview you and you get featured on the *Yahoo!* newsfeed. But there are "riches in niches," and you'll get more exposure and more results much quicker in media that is *specific* to your target audience.

DAY 8 – Who You Gonna Call? Your Perfect Media Match

~57~

3. Who's in Your Sweet Spot?

Who is your target market? It's not just the people who could benefit from what you have to offer (which could be just about anyone, right?), ***it's the people who would crave what you've got***—if they only knew about you! Specifically, what type of client or customer have you had the most success with? Those folks are your sweet spot, and you want to attract *more of them*.

4. What Are Your Sweet Spot's Sources?

Where do these people go for their entertainment, enlightenment or education?

Who do they trust? Are they magazines readers or early morning commuters?

Are they Internet savvy or television watchers?

And specifically, what publications, trade journals, radio shows, internet sites, or TV shows do they like?

5. What Are Your Strengths?

You may be perfectly willing and able to be interviewed on a talk show. You may be a fast and terrific writer who could churn out articles. Or you may be terrified to speak in public and can't write a lick! Though it's helpful to be prepared and available for *any* type of media, you may want to play to your strengths in the beginning.

6. Think Global, Start Local

Media begets media. As you begin your public relations campaign, cut your teeth and ***sharpen your skills with local media***. Make your mistakes—and learn from them!—with smaller audiences to prepare you for the larger ones. Build your media portfolio by appearing on local shows and in local publications.

7. Research Their Specific Wants and Needs

Once you've identified the best media vehicles to start with, do your research!

What types of guests do they have?

What types of articles or interviews do they feature?

What topics do they cover and who specifically covers them?

What's their "style?"

Actually watch or listen to the shows and read the publications you'll be pitching! (This, by the way, is one of those *key moves* that too few people do.)

DAY 8 – Who You Gonna Call? Your Perfect Media Match

~58~

8. Track Down Specific Contacts

You can often do this via the internet. Radio and TV shows will often list a producer. Publications have editors and by-lined journalists. Get not only a specific email for that person *and* a phone number. And if you can't find this info on their website, call the general number. Explain to the receptionist what type of benefit (story, insight, topic, etc.) you can offer and ask who you should contact. You can reach the media through their "contact us" website pages or you can email them. In addition to reaching them there, you can reach them through sites like Twitter, LinkedIn, Facebook, and YouTube.

9. Research Your Specific Ms. Media

Now that you have a specific contact, take some time to research that specific Ms. Media. Google her or him. Find out what other articles they've written or shows they've produced. To dramatically improve your odds of success, get to know them *before* you pitch them!

10. How Can I Help You Get Your Work Done Today?

As you do your research, whether it's the media venue or the specific contact person there, get yourself into the mindset of "How can I help them do their job?" How can you help entertain, enlighten or educate their audience? *How can you be a benefit to them?*

11. Prepare for Trial and Error

Not every pitch will land you a placement or an appearance. And not every placement or appearance will get you the results you want. Pay attention and keep track of what's working and what isn't. Then *keep doing what works!* What gets you more hits on your website? More inquiries via email? More calls to your office? That's where you want to spend your precious time.

DAY 8 – Who You Gonna Call? Your Perfect Media Match

~59~

Day Eight Action Steps

Let's start the hunt for your perfect media match!

1. ## Your Sweet Spot Avatars

   Begin finding your perfect media match by knowing precisely who you're trying to reach. Start by thinking of your current clients or customers, especially the ones you've had the most success with. Then describe at least 4 of them by age, gender, education, interests, concerns, dreams, and nightmares. (You can describe actual individuals or come up with a fictional composite.) What types of work do they do? How do they spend their free time?

   #1 _____

   _____

   _____

   _____

   _____

   _____

   _____

   _____

   _____

   _____

   _____

   _____

   _____

   _____

DAY 8 – Who You Gonna Call? Your Perfect Media Match

~ 60~

#2 _____

_____

_____

_____

_____

_____

_____

_____

_____

_____

#3 _____

_____

_____

_____

_____

_____

_____

_____

_____

_____

DAY 8 – Who You Gonna Call? Your Perfect Media Match

~61~

#4 _____

_____

_____

_____

_____

_____

_____

_____

_____

_____

2. What Do They Read, Watch, Listen To?

List their media sources. Where do they get their information, entertainment, inspiration? List as many sources as you can and be specific!

_____

_____

_____

_____

_____

_____

_____

_____

_____

_____

DAY 8 – Who You Gonna Call? Your Perfect Media Match

~ 62~

_____

_____

_____

_____

_____

_____

_____

_____

_____

_____

_____

_____

_____

3. Research 3 Good Media Options

Choose three of the specific media options you've chosen and begin your research. Read a few issues of the publication or watch the show a few times! Take notes on the following: What areas do they cover? Local, national, industry-specific, men's issues, etc. What specific topics do they feature? What expert resources do they choose as guests, for quotes, or as bylined authors? How long are their segments or articles? Where could I best fit their format and what they offer?

4. Find a Specific Contact Person

For each of your 3 good options, visit the website and/or call the general number to find out who your best contact person will be.

5. Begin Ms. Media's File

Open a file for each contact that includes your initial notes on their publication or show and their specific contact information. Google that person and add any personal or professional notes. Leave a place to keep track of when you contact them, what pitch you use, their response and your results.

DAY 8 – Who You Gonna Call? Your Perfect Media Match

~ 63 ~

DAY 8 – Who You Gonna Call? Your Perfect Media Match

~ 64~

DAY 9 – Asking for the First Date:
An Overview of Pitching

Okay, asking for the first date can be intimidating. It's like the dreaded cold call in sales—but only *if* you have the wrong mindset!

You are contacting Ms. Media to offer her real benefit, to make her job easier, to lighten her load! And you've done your research so you know who she is and just what she needs. You will *not* be a waste of her time but a valuable ally. You are a gift! So all we need to do is smooth out first contact.

We'll cover more specifics about the *written* (emailed) pitch over the next few days. Here, we'll give you an overview of pitching along with a few phone tips:

1. It's All About Timing

As you think about what to pitch, understand that different types of media operate on different timetables:

> *Magazines* will hunt for stories three to six months before that issue so they're interested in New Year's Day pitches in June or July).

> *Television* and *radio* set up schedules two to three weeks in advance though if it's *breaking news*, they often accept it that same day or a day ahead.

2. Start with Email, Follow Up by Phone

Almost everything is pitched via email in today's world! (We'll show you exactly how to write a killer email over the next few days.) But to be effective, your pitch needs a one-two punch: *First*, the dynamite email, *then* the follow-up phone call to let Ms. Media know that you've sent it.

3. No Attachment!

I'm not talking about the Buddhist perspective on life (though not being overly attached to results is a good idea with any PR campaign!). I'm saying *do not send attachments with this first email to Ms. Media*. Most of us have learned to be suspicious of attachments that come from people we don't know. Just seeing that your email has an attached file is often enough to get it instantly deleted.

DAY 9 – Who You Gonna Call? Your Perfect Media Match

~ 65 ~

4. Leave a Professional Voice Message

More often than not, when you follow-up you'll get Ms. Media's voicemail so script the message you'll leave ahead of time. Begin with a brief greeting then your name and contact information *slowly* so she can write it down. Next tell her what you have sent and why. Tell her *when* you sent it and *what subject line* to look out for. Thank her for her time and hang up! However. . .

5. Be Prepared for a Live Person!

Know exactly what you will say if Ms. Media answers! Tell her specifically why you are calling and why you are calling *her*. **Have your 30 second "elevator pitch" ready** (see below) and *be prepared* for a real conversation. If she says she's not interested in your specific pitch, thank her and ask her if there is any other way you might be helpful to her.

6. Your 30 Second Elevator Pitch

Basically, your "elevator pitch" presents

1. *who* you are,
2. *what* you do, and
3. *why* anyone should care

in a unique, compelling way in *30 seconds or less*.

A great elevator pitch sounds perfectly natural but is carefully crafted to get the most punch in the fewest words. (In the Appendix, you'll find several good examples to learn from. And once you've crafted your own, you'll practice it until you can say it in your sleep!)

7. Phone Etiquette

Ms. Media is extremely busy, but she's still a *person*. Whether on voice mail or in person, greet her warmly. *Smile as you talk* (a great trick that radio personalities and sales professionals use) and be glad to be talking to her! Especially if you're a bit nervous, slow down your pace of speech and speak clearly.

8. Short and Sweet

It's a fine balance. Whether leaving a message or talking in person, the trick is to be friendly and personable—but not so chatty that she dreads your calls. She's at work and working. If you can help with her work, great. If not, no harm, no foul *if* you've been respectful of her time.

DAY 9 – Who You Gonna Call? Your Perfect Media Match

~ 66~

9. Stay on Target

You are calling for a reason, so make sure that reason is clear. Don't be coy. Don't beat around the bush. After you greet her, say exactly why you're calling and specifically how you think you might assist her.

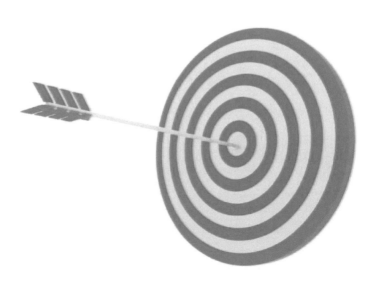

10. Get Personal

If you've done your research (you have, haven't you?), you've learned some things about Ms. Media's publication or show *and* some things about Ms. Media herself. Don't be afraid to compliment her most recent article or comment on a recent interview you enjoyed. This should be the sincere respect of one professional to another—no fawning allowed!

11. Any Other Way I Can Assist?

End each interaction with, "Please let me know if there's any other way I can assist you." This one line has opened countless doors! Maybe you can help with a different story. Maybe you know of a more appropriate resource for her. Maybe she needs a referral to an excellent Thai restaurant! By **being a giver, not a taker**, you become memorable to Ms. Media.

DAY 9 – Who You Gonna Call? Your Perfect Media Match

~67~

Day Nine Action Steps

They say that practice makes perfect. So let's set up some practice opportunities!

1. ## Write Your 30-Second Elevator Pitch

   Imagine this: Your plane has just landed and you're exiting the plane when, who do you spot? Oprah! You're about 5 feet from her seat where she is gathering her belongings. You're a big fan and you'd love to be on her show or in her magazine. You have 30 seconds to make an impression and get your message across. You take a deep breath, stick out your hand and say, "Hi, Oprah. . ."

   Create a 30 second (and yes, you need to *time* it!) elevator pitch that presents who you are, what you do and why someone should care. Use the examples in the Appendix to guide you.

   _____

   _____

   _____

   _____

   _____

   _____

   _____

   _____

   _____

   _____

   _____

   _____

   _____

DAY 9 – Who You Gonna Call? Your Perfect Media Match

~ 68~

_____

_____

_____

_____

_____

_____

_____

_____

_____

_____

_____

_____

_____

2. Rehearse, and Rehearse Some More!

Practice your elevator pitch until it feels as simple as saying your name or giving your birth date. If you keep stumbling over parts of it, modify the words until it sounds natural and comfortable. Practice while commuting. Practice in front of your cat. Practice while jogging. Practice while brushing your teeth. Try saying it as fast as you can, then with a goofy accent. Make it part of you!

3. Take It For a Test Drive

Once you feel somewhat comfortable with your elevator pitch, try it out on friend and colleagues to get their feedback. Use it to introduce yourself at parties or business functions. Be aware of the response you get. Do people seem intrigued? Confused? Put off? Bored? (Hint: You're hoping for "intrigued.")

DAY 9 – Who You Gonna Call? Your Perfect Media Match

~ 69 ~

DAY 9 – Who You Gonna Call? Your Perfect Media Match

~70~

DAY 10 – Give Her a Wink:
A Great Hook

Whether pitching in email or on the phone, the key to getting Ms. Media's attention is a great hook. What's a hook? It's like the juicy, shimmery, squiggly thing at the end of a fishing line that gets a fish's attention. It's the particular *approach* you use to connect to your expertise to your target audience.

For example, let's say you specialize in fitness for women over forty. You could get Ms. Media's attention with hooks like:

How to Get an Over-40 Bikini Bod in 3 Months, or
Energizing Exercises for Older Moms of Younger Kids, or
Exercises to Enhance Your Performance in the Boardroom, or
Exercises to Enhance Your Performance in the *Bed*room, or
Exercises that Reduce Blood Pressure and Increase Energy

Developing hooks and angles is similar to creating story ideas for your online press kit. Review the tips (News and Story Ideas) on page 30 and...

1. Study the Territory

Study the magazines, websites or shows you'll be pitching.

What hooks do they use regularly to present material?
How do they present the hooks? Do they use shocking statements? Intriguing questions?
Promises of amazing results?

Create your hooks to follow their lead and speak their same language.

2. Hook 'Em with the Big Six: Health, Wealth, Career, Sex, Relationships, Personal Growth

Most hooks will fall into these categories because these topics are what most of us care about and lose sleep over. These are the concerns that motivate us to action. Study how the media that serves your target market uses the Big Six. For example, a magazine geared toward men's health might feature an article on eating healthy foods with intriguing hooks like "healthy eating for better sex," "healthy eating to be sharper at work," or "healthy eating to prepare for your next marathon."

3. Drop a Delicious Hook, Not a Boring Net

A hook is *not* designed to grab *every*one. It catches the attention of particular fish. In fact, it's so irresistible to those specific fish that they feel, "Oh my gosh! How did they know? That's *exactly* what I need/want/have been thinking about!" A great hook motivates these fish to take the next step. A broad net (generic, non-targeted hook) inspires yawns, not action.

4. Be a Headliner

What's making front page news these days? What are the talking heads talking about? What are the sub-topics of these topics? How can you connect your expertise to those topics or sub-topics? Let's say the topic of the day is gun control and you teach meditation. How about "Breathing techniques that help you have sane discussions about gun control" or "Healing meditations for victims of violent crime"?

5. Turn Nightmares into Dreams

Our brains are on a constant quest to solve what we perceive as problems in our lives. Like heat-seeking missiles, our brains will instantly zoom in on anything that might be a solution for those problems. The best hooks *pinpoint a problem* and *promise a unique solution*.

6. Holiday Headaches

Oddly, every holiday, and season has its own set of problems or concerns, even if that concern is making it even more wonderful than last year. As that season or holiday approaches, we all begin to focus on these issues—the pressures of holiday entertaining, finding the perfect gift for Valentine's Day, dealing with Spring allergies, etc.—and so does Ms. Media.

7. Reuse and Recycle

The media calls it "re-purposing." It's your **same content** or message, but you dress it up **in different clothes**. For example, you might have content about health and beauty tips.

For summer, give it a sunny slant on tanning safely.

In winter, talk about how the cold and snow impact one's skin.

For Valentine's Day, explain how to give skin a romantic glow.

For a travel magazine, talk about travel-friendly skincare regimens.

8. Crank Up the Spice/Volume/Drama

Successful fishermen/women don't bait their hooks with dead, dull lures. Good lures have movement, vibration, flash, and color to entice their fish. So rather than "How to Help Kids with Homework," try "Skills Your Kids Need to Succeed in Life." Rather than "How to Date Online," try "The Secret to Finding Lasting Love and Happiness Online."

9. The Same But Different

Though you want hooks that are fresh and unique, ***don't worry about being totally original***. For the last 50 years, every women's magazine in the world has had articles on shedding weight to fit into our summer bathing suits. I guess that angle will still be hot in another 50 years! A hamburger is a hamburger. You don't need to (or *want* to) invent something *different* than a hamburger. You just want a hamburger that has some extra, unique sizzle!

Day Ten Action Steps

The good news is that you started this process when you came up with story ideas for your online press kit. Now let's hone your skill in creating great hooks to prepare you to pitch confidently to Ms. Media.

1. ## Watch a show or look at a publication that serves your target market.

   Jot down the hooks they use to introduce stories. What do you notice about these hooks?

   _____

   _____

   _____

   _____

   _____

   _____

   _____

   _____

   _____

   _____

2. ## Create hooks that connect you to your target audience.

   In this next exercise, brainstorm as many hooks as you can as quickly as you can in the following categories. Don't overthink this! Give yourself just one minute for each one:

   Hooks based on today's headlines:

   Headline: _____

   Hook: _____

Headline: _____

Hook: _____

Headline: _____

Hook: _____

Headline: _____

Hook: _____

Hooks based on the Big Six:

Health: _____

_____

Wealth: _____

_____

Career: _____

_____

Sex: _____

_____

Relationships: _____

_____

**Personal
Growth:** _____

_____

Hooks for holidays and seasons:

_____

_____

_____

_____

_____

_____

_____

_____

_____

3. **Now review all the hooks you brainstormed.**

Highlight the good ones. With slight re-working, could some of the others be attractive? Write your list of good possible hooks below.

_____

_____

_____

_____

_____

_____

_____

_____

_____

_____

_____

_____

_____

DAY 11 – In Three Sentences or Less: The Critical First Paragraph

By now, you're ready to turn your hook and story idea into a real-live pitch. As we mentioned, 99.99% of all pitches these days are done via email. If your email subject line is intriguing enough to keep Ms. Media from hitting the DELETE button (you'll learn to write killer subject lines on Day 13!), you want to maintain her interest in *every word and sentence* thereafter.

In writing books, they say that you either grab the reader with the first five pages or you lose them. In emailed pitches, it's your first **3 sentences** that **make or break you**. Those first 3 sentences will be slightly different depending on the type of media you're pitching. But they share some critical similarities:

1. We Got A Problem

State the problem or issue you're addressing **clearly within the first few sentences**. This is the problem side of the specific hook that you've developed. It may not be a problem for *everyone*, but it's a *significant* worry or concern for your target audience.

2. Are You a Match?

Does Ms. Media need and want what you have to offer? Help her figure that out within the first paragraph. Do this with a

QUESTION ("Are you looking for an expert who can tell parents how to navigate the treacherous world of college financing?") or,

STATEMENT ("Jocelyn Marks has helped thousands of people navigate the treacherous world of college financing.")

Within this one sentence, Ms. Media knows if you're a match for her audience and what she's working on.

3. Get to the Point

In the first few words of your pitch, get *immediately* to the point of what you can offer that Ms. Media can't get elsewhere. Remember to use short, snappy, concise sentences—no fluff.

4. Got Facts?

Ms. Media *loves* interesting *facts and statistics*! Rather than opening with, "Domestic violence is a serious problem," try "One in four women will experience domestic violence during her lifetime." Compare "A wedding is an expensive venture" to "The average wedding will cost $28, 671—more than most families pay annually for their mortgage!"

5. Compelling is the Key

Why they should care *must* be obvious in the first few sentences. Like creating your hooks, crank up the volume/spice/drama when writing your first paragraph. Make it interesting and compelling, not ho-hum.

Which catches your attention more, "People need to know more about their taxes" or "Every year, the average American pays thousands of dollars more than they need to in taxes"? Compare "There are many ways to have an income-producing business from home" to "Thousands of people have left the tyranny of the time-clock, the stress of daily commuting, and the agony of being at the boss's beck and call by creating, lucrative, and satisfying home-based businesses."

6. Pitching Breaking News

Ms. Media needs you to "advance the story," meaning *bring a new angle or deeper aspect* to the discussion. Begin with, "Do you need an expert to talk about XYZ?" then add to it. For example, "Do you need an expert to explain why the stock market just crashed and how investors can protect themselves?" or "Do you need an expert to discuss why football players like XYZ are prone to domestic violence and how victims can get help?"

7. Pitching a Season or Holiday

Begin with the holiday or season and the issue you address.

> "This Thanksgiving, wouldn't your busy readers love to know how to pull off the perfect, stress-free turkey dinner with all the trimmings?"

> "As April 15th approaches, we all want to be sure we're not paying more in taxes than we have to."

8. Pitching for Radio

Start with your topic or hook then follow it with why you're a great expert for that subject.

> "Every bride wants gorgeous hair for her wedding day. Brenda James, who has styled hair for top international models for decades, can explain exactly what you should and shouldn't do for perfect hair on the big day."

> "In this economy, it's difficult if not impossible for college grads to land decent jobs. George Karkis, a veteran professional recruiter for several Fortune 500 companies, can explain how new grads can beat the odds and land their dream job."

9. Pitching for Television

This pitch is similar to radio. But television is highly *visual* so focus on what **you can show** Ms. Media's audience. In your first paragraph, use words *like demonstrate, illustrate, display,* and *present.* (In the body of your pitch, you'll add even more visual ideas.)

10. Pitching to Magazines

Because of their long lead time, pitching to magazines is slightly different. To pitch seasonal hooks and topics, you need to approach editors at *least 3 to 4 months ahead of time*. And magazine stories need to be more evergreen, something that will be still pertinent to their readers months from now, not just today's flash-in-the-pan headline.

Begin your pitch to a magazine by mentioning a recent article they have run on a similar subject: "Your recent article 'Keep Your Child Safe at School' noted that bullying has become a primary concern in our school systems. Well-known child psychologist, Julian Lakin, has worked with thousands of children on both sides of the issue—both bullies and their victims. He offers practical advice to school professionals and parents on how to prevent bullying in all grade levels."

Day Eleven Action Steps

Today, we'll focus on creating those critical first 3 sentences. Pull out the hooks you developed on Day Ten. Choose at least five of them for the following exercises.

1. ## Write one sentence on the problem or issue.

   It can be a question or a statement. Remember to keep it compelling, brief, pointed.

   Hook: _____

   Problem sentence: _____

   _____

   Hook: _____

   Problem sentence: _____

   _____

   Hook: _____

   Problem sentence: _____

   _____

   Hook: _____

   Problem sentence: _____

   _____

   Hook: _____

   Problem sentence: _____

   _____

2. Write one sentence to establish you as an expert or credible source.

We're not looking for *all* of your credentials here. Just the one or two that proclaim "He/she can deliver!" on this *specific* topic. (You'll be able to expound on your credentials later in the body of the pitch.)

Hook: _____

Expert sentence: _____

_____

Hook: _____

Expert sentence: _____

_____

Hook: _____

Expert sentence: _____

_____

Hook: _____

Expert sentence: _____

_____

Hook: _____

Expert sentence: _____

_____

3. Write one sentence that is the overview of your unique offering.

By offering, I *don't* mean your product or service! It's the unique way you can enlighten, educate or entertain Ms. Media's audience on this topic.

Hook: _____

What I offer: _____

_____

_____

Hook: _____

What I offer: _____

_____

_____

Hook: _____

What I offer: _____

_____

_____

Hook: _____

What I offer: _____

_____

_____

Hook: _____

What I offer: _____

_____

_____

4. Put the three sentences you wrote for each hook together: problem sentence, expert sentence and what you offer.

Tweak them until they flow. Voila! You've got your first paragraph!

Hook: _____

3 Sentences: _____

_____

_____

_____

_____

_____

_____

Hook: _____

3 Sentences: _____

_____

_____

_____

_____

_____

_____

_____

Hook: _____

3 Sentences: _____

_____

_____

_____

_____

_____

_____

Hook: _____

3 Sentences: _____

_____

_____

_____

_____

_____

_____

Hook: _____

3 Sentences: _____

_____

_____

_____

_____

_____

_____

_____

Day 12 – A Beautiful Body:
The Meat of Your Pitch

You've caught her interest! Through your first 3 sentences, Ms. Media has determined that

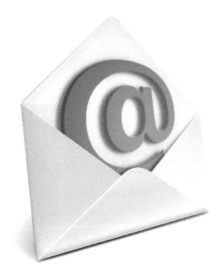

   a.   your topic might be of interest to her audience,
   b.   you're a match for what she's working on, and
   c.   you're a credible source.

Woo-hoo!

Now you need to bring it all home in the body of your pitch. In the body of the email, you'll give her more detail about your unique approach and perspective, your credentials and what you can offer her. Review the good email pitch examples in the Appendix with the following guidelines in mind:

1. Tell Her What You'll Tell Her

In the body of your email, don't be vague or general about what you bring to the table. Give the plot away, and let Ms. Media in on some specifics of how you will uniquely educate, entertain, and enlighten her audience about the topic or hook you've chosen.

2. Brevity is Still Key

Yes, you'll be giving more detail and yes, you need to get more specific. But the body of your email pitch must still be **under 300 words** (less than 200 is even better). Ms. Media doesn't have time to wade through more than that. And honestly?

If you can't explain your value in under 300 words, you probably aren't yet clear about what your value is! Choose your most unique, important, and interesting points. Leave out anything that's unnecessary, too common or obvious.

3. Bullets are Beautiful

One trick that will keep your writing sharp and your main ideas prominent is to **use bullet points** rather than standard paragraphs. A bullet point doesn't have to be a complete sentence. In fact, it shouldn't be more than 3 sentences—again, less is more! Each bullet point should contain just one intriguing concept or thought.

4. Secrets, Keys and Tips

Ms. Media *loves* these!

"Six Beauty Secrets from Top Models"

"The Three Keys to Re-financing Your Home"

"Twelve Tips to Make Your Holidays Brighter"

We're all looking for life hacks. We especially like them to be easy, simple, and practical. *And* we like them **numbered**! (Rather than "some tips," "twelve tips" sounds more definite and concrete.)

5. Tantalizing Tidbits

You don't have to give away all of your wisdom or explain all of your keys, tips or secrets. But do expand on one or two so Ms. Media sees how brilliant you are! Or if you have stories to share, give her a tease about some of them:

"Like the years she spent in the Playboy mansion, entertaining the likes of Robin Williams and Paul Newman."

"Following his coaching, one college grad landed a six-figure job at Disney and another was hired for his dream job at Google."

6. Garden Variety

Give Ms. Media some **choices** by letting her know a variety of topics you can speak about *or* the variety of ways you can speak about the same subject. For example, if your expertise is in helping students get into college, maybe you can talk about test scores, application essays or prepping for college interviews. Maybe you can discuss the subject of paying for college from the point of view of students, or parents, wealthy families or low-income families.

7. Give Her Some Gold

If you can, along with the tantalizing tidbits, give Ms. Media something specific she can *actually use*.

"Did you know that online daters who post professional photographs of themselves have a 52% higher success rate?"

"One simple key to good business decisions is to take ten deep breaths before you make a move."

8. What's In It for Them?

Ah, yes, we're all tuned into station WIIFM (What's in it for me?) Make sure it's very clear how your information or insight will benefit Ms. Media's audience keeping in mind the 3 E's (*educate, entertain, enlighten*). Can you help Ms. Media scoop her competition? Can you give her an exclusive or an entirely unique perspective?

9. All That and a Bag of Chips

Here's where you get to expand on your credentials beyond that one-line in the first paragraph. Since media coverage begets media coverage, let Ms. Media know where you've appeared or been featured. Tell her about your successes, specifically how you have helped folks just like her audience. Written a book? Won a prestigious award? Throw those in here.

10. How You Do What You Do

Do you have B-roll, charts, **graphics**? Do you have sound clips or specific **client stories** to share? Give her **links** to your materials. Are you humorous? Erudite? Controversial? Awesome at fielding audience questions? Give Ms. Media a sense of how you can present what you've got.

11. The When and Where of It

Do not forget to be *very clear* about when and how you are available. Are you available with less than 24 hour notice? Do you need to be booked months in advance (if so, don't expect tons of bookings!)? Are most of your interviews via phone? Can you travel and if so, what are your requirements (travel costs, etc.)? How does Ms. Media reach you?

12. The Big Easy

As you think about your availability and what you're willing and able to do for Ms. Media, keep this in mind: The more flexible and available you are, the more Ms. Media will be able to use you. If you have too many restrictions, she'll find someone else who is easier to work with—no matter how great you are!

Day Twelve Action Steps

Today, you'll build the body of your first pitch. Review the example pitches in the Appendix and the tips above.

1. ## Choose one of the hooks from Day 11 that you used to write the first paragraph and build a body for it.

   Fill in the blanks below.

   I'm sending this pitch to (type of media)

   _____

   My main points about this story/problem/issue (at *least* 3 presented in bullet points) are:

   1. _____

   _____

   2. _____

   _____

   3. _____

   _____

   The unique solutions or insights I bring (at *least* 3 presented in bullet points) are:

   1. _____

   _____

   2. _____

   _____

   3. _____

   _____

My additional credentials that make me uniquely qualified to speak to this issue are:

_____

_____

_____

_____

_____

My tantalizing tidbits or nuggets of gold include:

_____

_____

_____

_____

_____

How I can present this material:

_____

_____

_____

_____

_____

My best contact numbers and availability:

_____

_____

_____

_____

_____

2. **Take your responses above and make them as brief and crisp as you can.**
   Say what you have to say in the fewest words possible while still getting your points across in a compelling way.

   _____

   _____

   _____

   _____

   _____

   _____

   _____

   _____

   _____

   _____

   _____

   _____

   _____

3. **Put the body of your pitch with your first paragraph and have a trusted friend or colleague review it.**
   Does it catch their attention? Are they intrigued to learn more?

Day 13 – Open Sesame:
The Subject Line She Can't Resist

How many emails do you get in a day? Twenty? Fifty? Ms. Media gets *hundreds.* One TV producer we've worked with said he averages *1500 every 3 hours*! With that kind of volume and her hectic schedule, Ms. Media has developed a lightning-fast DELETE finger.

You don't want to get axed before she's seen your awesome pitch! The key is a subject line she can't resist.

1. Don't Be Spammy.

Spam has a certain fragrance, doesn't it? And most of us, consciously or unconsciously, have learned to recognize a spam email before we even open it by the language used in its subject line. Phrases like, "Act Now!" "Amazing Find!" or even "Don't Delete!" Your subject line can be compelling and intriguing **without a cheesy attempt** to create a false sense of urgency.

2. Hit the Headlines

Great subject lines are very much like great headlines. They give you a peek into the story (or email) *and* why it's important. Study headlines on newsfeeds, magazines or newspapers. Especially pay attention to the headlines or story intro's your particular Ms. Media uses. Notice which of these grab your attention and which fall flat. Model your subject line after the best ones.

3. Clever But Clear

Subject lines can be clever but not so clever that it leaves the reader confused rather than intrigued. Compare: "Beauty and the Beasts" to "Ways Tough Guys Can Look their Best." Or "Fried-Brain Hacks" to "4 Ways to Revive Our Stressed Brains." Which ones give you a clearer sense of the topic?

4. Use Her Key Words

Because she gets so many emails, Ms. Media often uses a key word search to find pitches that relate to the particular stories she's working on. Is she focused on health issues? She'll be looking for words like health, wellness, fitness, nutrition, etc. in the subject line.

Would she be focused on the latest breaking news story? If that's what your pitch is about, be sure to use words specific to that breaking news. Highlight your key words by putting them in parentheses.

5. Less Than a Sentence

Start with a few sentences that *summarize what is most important in your pitc*h. Pare that down to one sentence. Reduce that one sentence to **five words** or less. Presto! You've got a subject line!

6. Good, Not Perfect

Do *not* waste your time trying to create the absolute best subject line ever written! In fact, do not waste your time trying to create the most brilliant pitch in the history of PR. Honestly, to get Ms. Media's attention, your pitch, and subject line just have to be good *enough* and compelling *enough*. She is eager, even desperate, to find the material she needs. The purpose of your pitch is to help her find it—not to win the next Noble prize for literature.

Day Thirteen Action Steps

Okay, let's create some subject lines! Use the pitch you developed on Day Twelve for these exercises.

1. ## Create a pitch that summarizes your pitch's most critical points.

   Begin by writing a summary of those points in 2-3 sentences. Pare that down to one sentence. Finally, reduce that sentence to 5 words.

   2-3 sentence summary:

   _____

   _____

   _____

   _____

   _____

   One sentence:

   _____

   _____

   _____

   5 words:

   _____

   _____

2. Create a pitch that uses Ms. Media's key words.

Think about the key words your specific Ms. Media would use for this topic. Using the summary above, try to incorporate at least one of them.

_____

_____

_____

_____

3. Test market your subject lines.

Run your ideas by trusted colleagues or friends. Would they be interested in reading an email with any of your subject lines? What do they like and not like?

Day 14 – Just the Way Ms. Media Likes It:
Perfect Pitch Formula Formats

Ms. Media gets hundreds, if not *thousands*, of pitches per day. She needs to sort through them quickly to find the nuggets she needs for her audience. You can help her *tremendously* by following these standard formats that she's used to seeing. And, she'll instantly recognize you as a pro who knows the ropes of pitching the media!

So save your creativity for the content, and stick to these standard Pitch Formula formats.

1. Breaking news pitch formula

[Topic] Great subject line:

_____

Need an expert?

_____

_____

_____

_____

_____

Tips:

1. _____

2. _____

3. _____

4. _____

Geographic and date availability:

_____

_____

Phone number, email, after hours contact:

_____

_____

2. Seasonal/holiday/news pitch formula

[Season/holiday/news] Catchy subject line:

Mention season/holiday/breaking news.

Your unique commentary/content:

Geographic and date availability:

Phone number, email, after hours contact:

---

3. Radio pitch formula

[Topic] Catchy lead-in:

_____

Expert round-up intro:

_____

_____

_____

Ten questions host can ask you:

1. _____

2. _____

3. _____

4. _____

5. _____

6. _____

7. _____

8. _____

9. _____

10. _____

Geographic and date availability:

_____

_____

Phone number, email, after hours contact:

_____

_____

4. TV pitch formula

[Topic] Catchy lead-in:

_____

Expert round-up intro:

_____

_____

_____

_____

Three tips they can make into graphics:

1. _____

2. _____

3. _____

Geographic and date availability:

_____

_____

Phone number, email, after hours contact:

_____

_____

5. Magazine pitch formula

[Topic] Memorable headline:

_____

Mention a current article in the magazine that's related to your topic.

_____

_____

Suggest something you can speak about or write an article about.

_____

_____

_____

_____

Offer yourself as an expert who can be quoted or as a contributing writer.

_____

_____

_____

_____

Availability:

_____

_____

_____

_____

6. Internet pitch formula

Write a 500-to-800-word bylined article and submit it to Web portal editors. Check the website itself for submission guidelines and *follow* them! These guidelines may even tell you what to put in your subject line.

Article [Topic]: _____

Title: _____

By [Your name]: _____

Write an article that **educates** readers on a topic. This is not about promoting your service or product! Your article must give real value to readers to be considered.

_____

_____

_____

_____

_____

_____

_____

_____

_____

_____

_____

_____

_____

_____

_____

_____

_____

_____

_____

_____

_____

_____

_____

_____

_____

Byline: In this area you *can* promote by writing a short bio that is 3 sentences *max,* along with your Web site and email address. (Review tips for bylines in Day Four.)

_____

_____

_____

_____

_____

Day Fourteen Action Steps

Today's action steps are simple: Choose one or more of the pitch formats above and print them out. Using the material and ideas you've been generating this week, fill the forms with your very own pitches!

WEEK THREE – Reel 'em In: Out on the PR Campaign Trail

Time for the rubber to meet the road! If you've completed the action steps from the first two weeks (you have, haven't you?), then you have just about all you need to get together with Ms. Media up close and personal.

During this week, we'll show you **how to be a media darling** as well as make the most of the media coverage you land. You'll learn to create catchy and pithy sound bites and hone your story-telling skills.

Day 15 – The Gift of Gab:
Talking Points and Sound Bites

Remember Ms. Media's three main imperatives? (By now, they're probably tattooed on your forehead!) **Entertain**, **Educate**, and **Enlighten**. You've focused on these three in your press kit, your story ideas and your pitches. You're a pro!

But there's one last imperative you *must adhere to* when you actually land media coverage: Time. Whether you're featured in an article, or interviewed on radio or television, the time you have to make your points is *extremely limited!* Think in *seconds*, not minutes!

Magazine editors will give you very strict word-count guidelines. When you go into a radio sound booth, you'll see your interviewer "back timing," watching the clock to see just how many seconds before the next commercial break. Sets for TV shows have a producer or assistant counting down the seconds and signaling the host when it's time to "wrap it up." It doesn't matter how brilliant or entertaining or even famous you are, Ms. Media's time (or space) constraints are *not* negotiable!

So today, you'll focus on what Mark Twain called, "Minimum of sound to maximum of sense." Welcome to the wonderful world of sound bites!

1. Pithy Pleethe

Pithy is defined as "concise and forcefully expressive." That's exactly what you want to be when Ms. Media comes to call. To **prepare for different types of coverage**, you'll craft several sound bites, from one-liners to a few sentences. You should have a few 10-second, 20-second, 30-second, and 45-second snappy sound bites in your pocket and ready to go. (And yes, you really *must* time yourself!)

2. What's Your Point?

The first thing to figure out is, "What are the three or four most important points I want to make?" Truly *nailing* a few points is much more powerful than spewing out a zillion vaguely interesting thoughts. *Your important points may change with different topics* or angles. But do NOT sit down with Ms. Media before you know what your points are!

3. Unforgettable

A winning sound bite is *memorable*. Ms. Media and her audience may not recall everything you say, but your sound bites should be sticky, like that gum they can't quite get off their shoe. Compare these two:

#1 "The neurology of the brain is such that when you have a recurring thought, it causes the neuro-synapses to fire and that specific neuro-pathway becomes more easily activated so that you automatically revert to the thoughts you have most frequently."

#2 "When you think a thought frequently, your brain re-wires itself to *leap* to that thought automatically."

Which sticks with you? Yeah, me too.

4. Engage the Senses

A good picture really can be worth a thousand words! Make it visual as in this sound bite from Walt Disney: "There is more treasure in books than in all the pirate's loot on Treasure Island." Can't you immediately picture the gems and jewels? Or help them *feel* it, like this quote from Ronald Reagan: "When you can't make them see the light, make them feel the heat."

5. Pump Up the Emotion

We pay *much* more attention when our emotions are engaged. With emotion, we're not just processing information. We're processing how we *respond* to that information and the registers in our very cells. A great sound bite is often funny, poignant, irritating, or shocking. Here are a few from the masters:

"Live in such a way that you would not be ashamed to sell your parrot to the town gossip." (Will Rogers)

"Music was my refuge. I could crawl into the space between the notes and curl my back to loneliness." (Maya Angelou)

"What is absurd and monstrous about war is that men who have no personal quarrel should be trained to murder one another in cold blood." (Aldous Huxley)

6. Relatable

It seems like common sense, but many folks miss it: If you're talking to teenagers, use references, stories, analogies and words that *teenagers* relate to. This, of course, applies to any audience or group. That said, some things are universal. For example, we were all children at some point and we all had dreams as children. So a story about your own childhood dreams will touch most of us.

7. Use Analogies and Metaphors

These can be great tools for making your points sticky. Connecting your idea to *a common experience helps* it land solidly with your audience. Some examples: "I am to dancing what Roseanne is to singing and Donald Duck to motivational speeches. I am as graceful as a refrigerator falling down a flight of stairs." (Leonard Pitts) "Withdrawal of U.S. troops will become like salted peanuts to the American public; the more U.S. troops come home, the more will be demanded." (Henry Kissinger)

8. Facts and Stats

Facts and statistics are great tools for establishing credibility, and grabbing the audience's attention. They're especially powerful if they are surprising or shocking: "Obesity rates in the US have more than doubled since the 1970's." "Over 20% of all homeless people are US military veterans." "College tuition expenses have ballooned 1,225 % since 1978."

9. Carefully Crafted

We've urged you not to agonize and waste time trying to make your most of PR material perfect. "Good" for most things is good enough. HOWEVER, your sound bites and stories must be carefully crafted to get the impact you want. Use *verbs* that have *action*, *nouns* that have punch, *adjectives* and *adverbs* that give *dramatic color*.

10. Express Yourself

Even as you make your sound bites as spiffy as possible, they still have to sound like *you* because they'll be coming out of *your* mouth or under *your* byline. If you're an academic, not a rapper, forget the gangsta' language. Avoid fancy multi-syllabic words that make you trip over your own tongue. Craft sound bites that feel natural and conversational.

11. Practice and Practice then Practice Some More

You need to rehearse like crazy so your sound bite doesn't sound rehearsed! It's best to practice out loud, and even *better* to practice with someone else listening (your cat doesn't count). When you practice *with* someone, you're more likely to add intonation and eye contact. You'll be able to tell whether you feel confident and natural with your sound bites or still somewhat self-conscious.

Day Fifteen Action Steps

These exercises will help you draft your first 3 or 4 sound bites. Today, you'll focus on the shorter ones, 10 to 20 seconds.

1. Listen to the pros.

Tune in to a few talk shows and listen carefully to guests' responses. Notice what you like and don't like, what catches your attention and what loses your interest. Pay attention to the way really seasoned guests vary their responses from brief quips to slightly longer stories.

2. Take notes from the masters.

Visit websites like Brainy Quotes (www.BrainyQuote.com) or Good Reads (www.GoodReads.com/Quotes) and read quotes from a variety of authors. Notice which quotes grab you and analyze why they're good. (You can even memorize a few that are pertinent to your points—just make sure to credit the author!)

3. Find out how long 10-20 seconds can be.

Grab a timer with a second hand (your smartphone might have one). Time yourself saying several typical sentences to get the feel for how long 10 seconds and 20 seconds are. Unless you've been told that you are a very slow speaker, do *not* speed up your normal rhythm! Most people need to slow down in their delivery—especially when under pressure!

4. Create your own short sound bites.

For each sound bite, run all the way through the steps below. When you have a decent first draft, repeat the process with your next idea.

What's the big idea? Write down one important idea you'd like to present.

_____

_____

_____

_____

_____

_____

_____

Why is this a big deal? Jot down any significant, shocking or stunning stats or facts about this idea.

_____

_____

_____

_____

_____

Why should anyone care? What emotions could this point elicit?

_____

_____

_____

_____

_____

"It's just like . . ." See if you can come up with good analogies or metaphors for your idea. Relate your idea to everyday experiences, familiar images or bits of history, even TV commercials!

_____

_____

_____

_____

_____

Draft your point in one to four sentences.

_____

_____

_____

_____

_____

_____

_____

_____

Spice it up. Add color and movement with adjectives and action verbs. Compare "Stress is common in women during the holidays which leaves them fatigued later" to "Already frazzled moms slam into over-drive over the holidays—then crash and burn right after."

_____

_____

_____

_____

_____

_____

_____

_____

_____

Time it and trim it. Pay attention to any extraneous words that don't move the thought forward. Cut them out!

_____

_____

_____

_____

_____

_____

_____

_____

_____

Jot your sound bite down on a 3 X 5 that you can keep with you. Practice it over and over. Try it out on colleagues and friends then refine it.

Day 16 – Scheherazade's Secret: Become a Great Storyteller

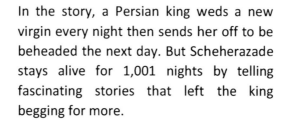

Do you remember the story of Scheherazade?

In the story, a Persian king weds a new virgin every night then sends her off to be beheaded the next day. But Scheherazade stays alive for 1,001 nights by telling fascinating stories that left the king begging for more.

She was **a phenomenal story-teller!**

And to stay alive with Ms. Media, you want to become one as well. To tell terrific, sticky stories, make sure to use all of yesterday's tips too!

1. Make a Point

It's true that big celebrity guests can get away with just sharing gossip or telling funny stories. You probably can't. While you want to be entertaining, be sure your stories also **make a point** that will enlighten or educate Ms. Media and her audience. Just like your shorter sound bites, your stories should make a maximum of sense using a minimum of sound.

2. 45 Seconds—or *Less*

Even though you get a *few* more moments to tell a great story, keep it brief. To help you do so, a few pointers:

Don't start at the very beginning. We usually don't need much background.

Cut out all um's and uh's, and any other "stalling" words (anyway, well, so, by the way, etc.).

Don't waste your words stating the obvious or unnecessary. By definition, a baby is young, a great grandmother is old, and the sun shines.

Get on the road and follow it! Avoid wandering off into side alleys that have nothing to do with your story or point. Use the next 4 steps to keep you on track.

#1 Begin with The Set Up.

Start by giving the context of your story. Tell them when, where and who—but only if those details are important to the story. It can be as brief as, "When I was a child, I had horrible vision but nobody knew it. I didn't know what I couldn't see and, because I was a good listener and very smart and resourceful, nobody else figured out that something was wrong." We don't need to know that you grew up in New Jersey with two brothers and a sister and a dog named Clyde *unless* those details will be critical to the rest of the story.

#2 Proceed with The Action.

What happens next? Remember, you're on a specific road so *each action should lead directly to the next action* down that specific road. "But when I hit grade school, I started getting notes on my report card that I was extremely shy. Though she's highly intelligent, she never volunteers to respond in class.' When I started reading, my mom noticed that I keep my nose 6 inches from the page. It finally dawned on someone that we should get my eyes checked. So we headed to the optometrist."

#3 Get to The Result.

This is the place *all* those *actions lead to*, where the good guy rides off into the sunset or the heroine is released from the evil curse. "It turns out that I was virtually blind. The optometrist said I was 'twenty-two fingers,' meaning I could barely see two fingers in front of my nose. When he put glasses on me, it was if an entire world opened up that I didn't know existed."

#4 The Moral of the Story.

Just as in life, you can draw a zillion different conclusions from just about any story. For example, the story about the near-sighted little girl could conclude with "We don't know what we can't see until we see it" or "Children are incredibly resourceful but often to their detriment" or "It's easy to misdiagnose eye problems in pre-school children."

Craft the moral of *your* story into one of the main points you're trying to make.

3. Give Us Some Drama.

A story can be *simple*. But it needs a *little drama or surprise to* keep our interest. We want someone to overcome a challenge or do something out of the ordinary. A story about a guy who goes to a job interview, does well then gets the job is pretty boring. But the one where he misses the bus, has to run all the way to the interview, spills his coffee down his shirt, runs breathless into the wrong room and interrupts six executives, blurts out why he's perfect for that position and *then* gets the job—well, that's a story!

To get that kind of drama, you may have to exaggerate just a bit. But whatever you do, DO NOT make it all up and try to sell it as true! The fall from that pedestal can be deadly.

4. Keep It Personal.

One more note about *good stories: often* the best ones are *very personal*. We are attracted to (and trust) vulnerability. So even if you're telling a story about someone else, the more personal it is, the more impactful it will be. Stories that begin with "A guy walks into a bar" might make a good point. But they won't have the emotional punch a real story can have.

5. Rehearse Then Rehearse Some More

As well-known character actor Donald Pleasence said, "All the *real* work is done in the rehearsal period." Once you've crafted your stories, you *must **practice them over*** and over until they become part of you. Rehearse in front of others. Record your rehearsals and play them back. If you aren't used to rehearsing like this, it may feel a bit silly and unnecessary. But once the cameras zoom in and mics are hot and you're face to face with Ms. Media, you'll be grateful that you did! Even telephone interviews can be disconcerting in the beginning. With great preparation, you won't flub your key points under pressure.

DAY 16 – Scheherazade's Secret: Become a Great Storyteller

Day Sixteen Action Steps

Let's put together some Scheherazade-worthy stories. All of your stories should be under 45 seconds, the briefer the better! Pay attention to the 4 steps: #1 Set Up, #2 Action, #3 Result, and #4 Moral or Insight.

1. ## Looking at your main points, think of stories from your own life or stories of others.
    Which stories could apply to which points? Without judging, jot them all down.

    _____

    _____

    _____

    _____

    _____

    _____

    _____

    _____

    _____

    _____

    _____

    _____

    _____

2. ## Note which stories are unusual, interesting, unique or striking.
    Put an asterisk next to those. Which of the stories are very personal or poignant? Funny or shocking? Mark those as well.

3. ## Using all of the tips from the past two days, craft a few of these stories into good ones.

    Time yourself and make sure they really are under 45 seconds *without* speeding up your speech.

4. ## Set up a practice routine.

    Try outlining your story on 3 X 5 cards with key words. Stand in front of the mirror or sit in front of a camcorder. Work with each story until you are comfortable with it.

5. ## Take your stories on a test drive.

    After you've practiced each story, start telling it to friends or colleagues. What kind of response do you get? How could you modify that story to be more powerful? Tweak each one as needed and try again.

Day 17 – Act Like a PR Pro:
How to Be Ms. Media's Darling

You've done all this work to land a media placement! Maybe you're being interviewed for a magazine article or joining the morning zoo hosts on local radio or appearing on a talk show. However big or small, let's make sure they end up wanting more of you!

1. Do Your Homework

Usually, you'll have a little time to *research Ms. Media's particular vehicle*. Read, watch or listen to understand what she typically wants from her guests or contributors. Pay attention to topics, style, and format. How much time are guests given? Who takes the lead in the discussion?

2. Be Professional

Show Ms. Media that you take her seriously. Be on time (or early!) and have your act together. Be dressed appropriately and well-rehearsed on your topic. If she requested materials in advance, send them on time *and* bring copies with you. If you have to cancel or re-schedule, give her as much lead time as possible— or better yet, find her an excellent replacement! If you are *not* reliable and professional in all ways, as far as Ms. Media is concerned, you're history!

3. Prepare for the Unexpected

Stuff happens in life and in Ms. Media's world, stuff happens all the time. Her internet is down so she can't Skype you for the interview. Late-breaking news pushes her line-up (and you) into next week. A scoop from another source means your angle no longer applies. The producer loses your B-roll and they can't find your bio.

If you really want to be Ms. Media's BFF, follow the Boy Scout motto and **be prepared!** Have your B-roll and your graphics on a zip drive. Bring extra copies of any printed materials. Have all of her phone numbers (and make sure she has yours) so you can reach each other in an emergency. Leave extra time before and after your appointed "time slot" in case the schedule changes. And whatever happens…

4. Be Flexible!

Have you ever planned a date with someone special or an outing with friends only to have all your carefully laid plans fall apart? And who do you remember fondly from those times? The one(s) who remained calm and pleasant, who didn't whine or blame but went with the flow and took some of the pressure off you, right? Maybe they even helped you solve the problems or came up with totally different ideas to make the time rewarding.

When your experience with Ms. Media doesn't go exactly as promised or planned, staying flexible can turn a potential disaster for her into a win for both of you! (That said, if that particular Ms. Media always seems to be in crisis or never delivers what she promises, you might politely bow out to not waste your time.)

5. Connect with the Crew

In Ms. Media's world (like all businesses), the un-sung support staff is what makes the show go on. Her assistants, sound guys and gals, camera people, make-up artists—all of them play a critical role. They've seen it all and done it all. And if you treat them with the respect and consideration they deserve, they will bend over backwards to make sure you shine.

6. Make Ms. Media Look Good

From Day One, we've explained that your mission is to serve Ms. Media, not to be served by her. She has chosen you so prove to her that you were a good choice. Even if the interview is an adversarial one (which is rare unless that's what you're going for!) or the interviewer is unprepared (which actually is not so rare), show respect for who she is, the questions she asks and the comments she makes.

7. Remember Your Mission

Your mission is NOT to promote yourself, your product, your book or your service! Your mission (say it with me) is to **Entertain**, **Educate**, and **Enlighten** Ms. Media's audience. To help keep you on track with that mission, *don't* think of the audience as potential clients or shoppers. Imagine them, as students in a classroom or people coming to see a show. See them commuting in their cars, needing a lift to their day or some insight into a concern. ***Focus on giving*** them something valuable, not what you might get in return.

8. Listen and Respond.

Don't be so enamored or rigid with your sound bites and talking points that you can't have a real conversation with Ms. Media! Is there anything more irritating than a guest who won't respond to what an interviewer is asking? Ms. Media picks certain questions based on what she knows her audience is interested in. If you *don't know how to answer* her questions, ***say so***. Then do the best you can to *provide information* or insight that is related to what she's asked.

9. Prepare for Different Media

Ms. Media takes several forms. Much of your preparation up to this point (studying the format, prepping sound bites and stories, etc.) applies to all of them. Here are a few additional tips that are specific to each vehicle:

i. Radio

Often radio interviews are done via phone which is great because you can be in your jammies and have all your notes right in front of you! When setting up the interview, be clear about whether they will call you or you will call them. Have alternate numbers just in case you can't connect for some reason. If using a cell phone, make sure it's charged up and your reception is good. Disconnect your call waiting (on most systems, you do this by pressing *70) and make sure you won't be disturbed by dogs barking, children screaming or colleagues knocking on your door.

ii. TV

For this, you need to get dressed! Watch the show and pay attention to what the host and other guests wear. In general, bright white, lots or stripes, or ziggy patterns do not do well on camera. Avoid jewelry that might clink and clatter when you move. Wear something that makes you feel comfortable and confident!

Typically, you'll do your own make-up (bring extra along for touch-ups). Make sure you have clear directions to the studio and know how to get in (leaving extra time to get through security).

iii. Print

If asked to submit an article, adhere to their guidelines carefully and pay attention to the style of other articles they've published. Make sure you understand exactly what topic they want you to cover. When interviewed as part of someone else's article, respond promptly so they can meet their deadline (either by phone or email). Give the interviewer several short, snappy sound bites they can use as quotes from you. Offer statistics or other expert knowledge you have on the subject. The more helpful you are, the more likely Ms. Media will think of you when her next article comes up.

Day Seventeen Action Steps

If you've done your action steps from the past few days (as I'm certain you have!), you've done most of the heavy lifting in terms of preparation for Ms. Media's call. So today's action steps are easy:

1. Choose your TV outfits.

Go through your closet and find one or two "go to" outfits for your upcoming television appearances. Make sure that they reflect who you are and that you feel comfortable and confident in them!

2. Organize your sound bites and stories.

Consider putting together a binder of your sound bites and stories for phone interviews and for your on-going rehearsal. Organize them by topic or in whatever way makes sense for you. Make sure the print is large enough that you can find what you need easily. Continually add more stories and sound bites to keep what you have to say fresh and interesting.

Day 18 – After Your Date:
Building on Success

So your hard work has paid off, and you've just had your first date with Ms. Media! Woo-hoo! But this is not the time to sit back sipping piña coladas on the beach. Don't drop the ball! To get the most out of this date—and all media moments in the future—pay attention to the following tips:

1. Follow Up, Follow Through

Whether the date was great or not so great, follow up with a **sincere thank you note** or email. A little appreciation is very memorable, and you *do* want her to remember you when other opportunities arise! If Ms. Media asked for any additional material, send it promptly. Even if she didn't ask, if you have something that would be helpful her, send it along.

2. Maintain the Relationship

Now that you and Ms. Media have made a connection, *pay attention* to what she's up to. Shoot her a note of congratulations if she gets promoted. Let her know when you especially like a piece she presents. Offer her tidbits and insights into what she's covering or *offer her story ideas*. You don't need to contact her constantly (that's called stalking) but drop her a line when you have something worthwhile to offer.

3. Capture the Moment

If your media moment was on television, be sure to record it so you can **post a link to it in your press kit**. (You can post the video on YouTube or your website and link it from there.) If it was radio or a webcast, capture the audio and do the same. Put it on your website. Post the *link on Facebook* and *Tweet about it*. Were you quoted in an article or wrote one yourself that was published? Grab those articles and post those as well.

4. Learn from Your Mistakes

Even if you were great, we can *always* be better! Listen to or watch yourself. Re-read that article or blog. Without being overly critical, what could you tweak or improve for next time out? Ask trusted colleagues or friends for feedback as well. You can even ask Ms. Media herself for any constructive criticism when you send that thank you.

An important note: What if you blew it your first time out? Your hands shook like crazy, you forgot all your sound bites, and sweat drenched your shirt? Excellent! Now the worst is over and you can only go up from here! Seriously, rather than changing your name and moving to Patagonia, pick yourself up, dust yourself off, and figure out what you need to do to improve whatever tripped you up. Interacting with Ms. Media is a significant step that few have the courage to take. Congratulate yourself for that courage and forge ahead!

5. Pitch Again NOW

The best time to ask for more dates is right after you've had a great (or not-so-great) date! You've already successfully landed one media placement, so *know* you can land another. **Pull out** your **pitches** and **send them to new Ms. Medias**. Or create some new pitches. Pay attention to what worked in the pitch that landed you a placement and do more of that!

6. Drop Some Names

We always want what someone else has, right? Well, Ms. Media is more interested in you when you've "dated' her cousins! Mention your recent placement in your pitches. "As I said on my interview with XYZ" or "In the article I wrote for XYZ." You can even use the infamous, "As seen on XYZ TV!"

7. Ready for Bigger Arenas?

When you are just starting out, it helps to shoot for smaller venues. First of all, *it's easier to get a placement in smaller, local shows* or publications. And it not only gives you valuable practice in front of a smaller (perhaps less intimidating) audience, but it also starts building your street cred. *Once* you've *appeared* locally a few times, *consider* pitching to Ms. Media on the *regional or even national level.*

8. Get Organized!

We all have different ways to organize our contacts. Some people use spreadsheets, others have a Rolodex, still others have sophisticated contact management systems. Set up whatever works for you to maintain Ms. Media's contact information, pitches you sent her, notes on placements you had with her, when and how you followed up, etc. Do not trust your memory! Once you get rolling, you'll have several Ms. Medias to juggle!

Day Eighteen Action Steps

Even if you haven't had your first date with Ms. Media, you can get prepared because that day *will* come!

1. ## Organize your data bank for Ms. Media.
   Figure out whatever system works for you and set it up, populating it with people you've sent pitches to and the "dates" you've already landed.

2. ## Figure out how to capture your media moments.
   Research YouTube and the capacity of your press kit and website. Set up a page in your press kit for Media Placements. Decide how to feature your media appearances on your website.

3. ## If you've had a date, follow the tips above to get the most mileage out of it!
   If you haven't already, send a thank you to Ms. Media. Follow up and follow through in any way that is appropriate. Post your media moment on your press kit, website, and Facebook page.

Day 19 – The Gift That Keeps On Giving: Leverage Your PR

It's true that media begets media. But it can beget a heck of a lot more than that! And honestly, you started down this road aimed at more than just getting a good tan in the limelight, didn't you? So now is the time to think about the **real benefits** your budding **relationship with Ms. Media** can give you.

1. Book Deal.

This is like that chicken or egg dynamic: Which comes first? Authoring a book can help get you Ms. Media's attention—but Ms. Media's attention can also get you a book deal. By tailoring their campaigns, many people have successfully leveraged their media activity into publishing deals. If this is your goal, first go for some awesome media moments. Then use those media moments to pitch your book idea to literary agents and publishers.

2. Speaking Gigs.

Your street cred on the speaking circuit rises *dramatically* when you've been in Ms. Media's spotlight. People who book speakers need a great reason to choose you over someone else—and being the expert that Ms. Media chooses is a terrific reason! Television appearances are especially persuasive because the booker can get a clear sense of your style and how well you present your points. Be sure to include links to your clips in any speaker packages you send out.

3. Your Own TV or Radio Show.

If this is your goal, catching Ms. Media's attention is a great launch pad. We live in an age of inexpensive, high-value digital production equipment and zillions of channels and outlets that need programs. With some focus, persistence, and effort, becoming a community celebrity or internet star is very attainable. And with more focus, persistence, and effort, you could be picked up nationally to become the next Dr. Oz or Kelly Ripa. Heck, if Honey Boo Boo can get her own show, why not you?!

4. Business Ventures

Your PR campaign can be leveraged into a variety of business ventures. Your media moments can attract business partners or financial support to an idea you already have. Or someone could recognize that you and your expertise would be the perfect complement to their business idea. You could be tapped to be the spokesperson for someone else's company or product. You could be asked to consult on a project or recruited to teach a seminar or class. When people know about you—and see that you have Ms. Media's blessing—they can come up with all kinds of possibilities for you.

5. Your Best Calling Card

Bottom line: Your media moments *establish credibility* and can open all kinds of doors for you. Want to be on that prime-time panel at your annual industry conference? Send the committee your clips and articles. Aiming to increase your rates or focus on a different type of clientele? Media exposure positions you as the expert who can charge more and be pickier about clients.

6. Share with Clients

Exposure through Ms. Media not only attracts new clients, it can enhance your relationship with existing clients and customers. Send them links to your audio or video clips. Email them articles you've written or are featured in. Their good opinion of you will be that much better and they'll feel special to know someone Ms. Media favors. As an added bonus, they'll feel great referring others to you!

7. Spread on Social Media

You don't have to be a social media master to make sure your media moments are posted on Facebook or LinkedIn. And you never know who will pick up— and pass on—your Tweets and posts.

And don't forget that you have to be an avid commenter and re-tweeter. Build your community and not only share you PR presence. If you do so, your audience will be very generous. They will spread your news, they become your voice, and then only the (social media) sky is the limit

8. Repurpose

Everything you do for and with Ms. Media can *and should* be used in other formats! Post clips of your guest appearances on your website and on your press kit. Take an article you've written for one publication and redraft it using different analogies or examples for another publication or your own blog (The ideas can be the same. But DO NOT submit a published article to another publication without changing it up!). Were you a featured guest on a panel? Get the transcript and turn it into an article or blog.

Day Nineteen Action Steps

Are you starting to get the larger picture of the doors Ms. Media can open for you? And how you can get much more mileage out of your media moments? Let's capitalize on this leverage in your action steps today.

1. Consider potential opportunities that Ms. Media could offer.

Is it a book deal, a new business, your own show? Take a few moments to jot down possibilities you may not have considered before. Which feel exciting to you? Are any of them worth focusing on right now?

_____

_____

_____

_____

_____

_____

_____

_____

_____

2. What are some practical ways you can leverage your current media moments right now?

Post your articles and video and audio clips to your website and press kit, to Facebook and LinkedIn. (If you're not sure how to do this, your first step is to ask someone or go online and find out!)

3. Create an ongoing PR leveraging system for yourself.

For example, set up a group list of clients so you can send out clips of your appearance. Or set up a file of published articles that could be rewritten and submitted to other publications. Determine a reasonable time schedule for doing this, i.e. "I'll rewrite each article within one week of its publication and submit it to another vehicle within the month." Make your system easy and repeatable—and devise reminders for yourself.

DAY 20 – Are We There Yet?
Re-evaluate Your PR Campaign

So you've had your first date or several dates with Ms. Media. And you've done everything we suggested— so she likes you! She really likes you!

Now's the time to figure out where this relationship is going and what you really want from it.

1. PR Pitfalls.

Now that you've really gotten to know Ms. Media, you might have seen some traits that are tricky to deal with. Maybe her demands on your time have cut into your family or production time more than you're comfortable with. Maybe *her* deadlines cause you to miss your own. Maybe it's become expensive to meet her on her turf or to send the materials she wants. Most issues you've encountered are resolvable through scheduling, getting support, etc. But you need to be very clear about the issues first.

2. Your Strengths

By now, you've got a good idea of how well or how easily you can meet Ms. Media's desires. Perhaps it's a no brainer to whip out a 500-word article for her. But you still get the hives and go totally blank when that sparkly, bubbly TV host asks you an unexpected question. Strengths can be strengthened and weaknesses overcome. But start by being honest **about where you are** now that you have some experience under your belt.

3. The Enjoyment Factor

Life is supposed to be fun—or at the very least, *not* miserable! And honestly, do we really keep up with activities we hate? Spin class at 6AM may sound like the fastest way to your fitness goal. But if you hate doing it, how likely are you to stay committed? An ongoing relationship with Ms. Media requires enthusiasm and energy. So ask yourself, in your activities with Ms. Media, what have you really enjoyed? (Do more of those.) What activities have you consistently dreaded? (Figure out if they're really needed or if someone else could cover them.)

4. Your Results.

Again, most people don't engage Ms. Media to become a celebrity simply for celebrity's sake. On Day One, you were specific about what you hoped to gain from your PR campaign. You've given Ms. Media what she wants. Now is she giving you what you want? Are you selling the books or widgets you want to sell? Getting the new clients or donors you want? Have any new, possibly better opportunities opened up because of your relationship with Ms. Media? Are you *getting* enough to justify all that you are *giving*?

5. Your Sweet Spot

You'll find that your sweet spot, that place where you're firing on all cylinders, is a **combination of**

- your strengths,
- what you enjoy, and
- what gets you the best results.

Think about your career or business: Your sweet spot may be doing one-on-one coaching with clients or coming up with innovative product ideas. But other activities—maybe bookkeeping or blogging on your website—aren't in that zone. Are you doing things in your relationship with Ms. Media that are *not* in your sweet spot? Do these things really have to be done or could someone else do them?

6. Is This For You?

As you've seen by now, a relationship with Ms. Media takes some commitment and effort. In many ways, it gets easier as you get systems in place and you become more skilled at the PR dance. But while PR can be highly rewarding on many levels, it isn't for everyone. And it may not be appropriate for this particular time of your life or your business.

7. Set New Goals

If you've decided that an ongoing relationship with Ms. Media *is* for you, now is the time to set new goals. You've gotten a taste of what she can provide you and you have a better sense of what is realistic and doable. And you've probably had your eyes opened to new possibilities.

Day Twenty Action Steps

If you've been working all of your action steps, the last couple of weeks have probably been a flurry of activity! But take a moment now, step back and use the questions below to evaluate just where you are so far with Ms. Media, *and* where you want to go next.

(It's early days and you may not have had a lot of media moments yet. If so, you may want to hold off on this exercise and re-evaluate when you've had more experience being up close and personal with Ms. Media.)

1. What issues or challenges have I run into?

_____

_____

_____

_____

_____

_____

_____

2. How could I resolve those issues?

_____

_____

_____

_____

_____

_____

_____

3. **What are my strengths so far with Ms. Media?**

4. **How can I strengthen those strengths?**

5. **What are my weaknesses so far?**

6. **Do I need to and want to strengthen them? And if so, how will I do it?**

_____

_____

_____

_____

_____

_____

7. **What PR activities am I really enjoying?**

_____

_____

_____

_____

_____

_____

8. **What PR activities do I hate?**

_____

_____

_____

_____

_____

_____

9. **Are the activities I don't like really necessary? If so, can I get support in doing these things or delegate them to someone else?**

_____

_____

_____

_____

_____

10. **Am I getting the results I'd hoped for on Day One? Am I getting other positive results that make my time and effort worth it?**

_____

_____

_____

_____

_____

11. **How can I do more in my sweet spot (i.e. the things I'm really good at and enjoy and that get great results)?**

_____

_____

_____

_____

_____

12. **Are the goals I set on Day One still valid? Which ones would I change or delete? What goals would I add?**

_____

_____

_____

_____

_____

_____

_____

_____

_____

Day 21 – You've Got the Ball Now Don't Drop It: Create Your Sustainable PR Plan

You've evaluated your relationship with Ms. Media and decided that, though it may need some tweaks, it's a relationship worth continuing. If you're going for happily ever after and 'til death do us part, your relationship with Ms. Media needs to find its place within the rest of your life.

1. Game Plan

Now's the time to come up with a PR game plan to maintain the momentum you've started. Though you may have certain times where you'll want to push a bit harder—like for a new book, or launching a new product or project—your basic PR game plan must be sustainable over the long run. Like any relationship, you can't expect to ditch Ms. Media *completely* for months or years then pick right back up where you left off! She requires at least **some ongoing attention**.

2. Think Bite-size

The most sustainable PR plans stay relatively small and can fit comfortably into the rest of your work and family life. For example, rather than maintaining relationships with fifty Ms. Media's of various types and styles, choose only 10 media contacts to keep in touch with on a regular basis. You might be able to land a TV interview twice per week, but twice per month may be more realistic based on the time you have and everything else you need to do. Create your bite-size PR plan around your sweet spots (strengths, most enjoyable, best results).

3. Form a Team

Like any DIY venture, you can still do a do-it-yourself PR campaign without doing it *all* yourself! Figure out what support you need and how much it's worth to you. Maybe you need someone to keep track of schedules, or do research for interviews, or write your articles or blogs. Maybe you need a counterpart to cover clients while you're off with Ms. Media. Figure out what support would give you the biggest bang for your buck.

4. Find a Pro

If you are serious about public relations but don't have the capacity to do all the legwork yourself, consider hiring a pro. Seasoned PR firms already have good, established relationships with Ms. Media, and they know where you are most likely to get the coverage and results you desire. Besides their ability to "smile and dial" Ms. Media for you, they can advise you on everything from how your head shots should look to which media outlets will give you the most traction.

Get references for PR firms from people you trust. Compare prices but, as importantly, interview a few firms to make sure you find a good fit. Ask them to be clear about what they will do for you and what you can expect.

5. Track Your Results

Whether you stick with the DIY approach or hire a PR pro, you want to capture two types of results. One is how often you caught Ms. Media's attention: how often you were quoted in articles, or invited to do a TV or radio show based on your pitches. The second result to track is, how did that media attention translate into sales or new clients or whatever business results you're seeking?

6. Ongoing Learning

You've learned a heck of a lot over the past 21 days! But like any industry, **PR is continually changing and growing**. Two decades ago, press kits were mailed by snail mail—or in emergency, faxed!—and no one had even heard of Facebook or Twitter. To stay effective, keep your ears and eyes open to new PR trends, vehicles, and opportunities. And, to stay on Ms. Media's radar, continue to hone your skills to *become an even better guest/blogger/panel expert*.

Day Twenty-One Action Steps

It's said that a goal is just a wish unless it has a plan attached to it. Now that you've gotten your feet wet, you're ready to draft a PR plan that will be sustainable going forward and get what you want from your relationship with Ms. Media.

1. List your goals.

Begin with your goals of what you're trying to achieve through your PR campaign (i.e. number of widgets sold, clients gained, a book deal, etc.). Next list your PR goals (how many articles placed or guest appearances, etc.). Make sure all of your goals have specific timeframes or dates for completion.

_____

_____

_____

_____

_____

_____

_____

_____

2. Decide how much time you can devote to Ms. Media.

Based on what you have going in your life, how much time can you reasonably spend on your PR plan? Make sure you feel comfortable devoting this amount of time on a consistent, continual basis.

3. What is the best use of the time you can devote?

What are the most important things *you* should be doing? Again, think of your sweet spots.

4. ## What kind of support do you need and what resources do you have?

Think of people who are really good at what you don't have time for or are not good at. If you don't know anyone personally who could help, where might you find a useful resource? Consider both paid and unpaid help.

_____

_____

_____

_____

_____

_____

_____

5. ## Get references to professional PR firms.

You may or may not go this route, but at least get some indication of what a PR firm could offer you, the range of what it would cost, and whether it might be a good option now or in the future.

_____

_____

_____

_____

_____

_____

_____

6. ## Determine or design a tracking system.

    Track not only how many placements you get for the pitches you send out but also the results to your business itself.

    _____

    _____

    _____

    _____

    _____

    _____

    _____

7. ## Create your own continuing education plan.

    Where would you like to improve? If you want to be a better speaker, how about joining a Toastmasters' Club? Need better information on your industry? How about subscribing to the blogs or publications of other experts in your field?

    _____

    _____

    _____

    _____

    _____

    _____

    _____

    _____

    _____

    _____

    _____

Appendix – Inspiration and Guidance:
Examples of Success

Home Page Examples

Welcome to the online press kit for The Hendricks Institute, Inc.

After 34 years of marriage, bestselling authors Drs. Gay and Kathlyn Hendricks, Ph.D., know well that cultivating a healthy love relationship is an ongoing commitment. Their new book opens the doorway to thriving in love at midlife and beyond

Conscious Loving Ever After

Twenty-three years after the release of their smash-hit bestseller "Conscious Loving," Drs. Gay and Katie Hendricks, Ph.D., are once again making major waves in the way the world understands love. Their new book, "Conscious Loving Ever After," teaches people how to nurture relationships in midlife through elderhood and offers valuable insight to singles and couples both gay and straight. Over the years, these leaders in the relationship field have turned their own relationship into what they call a "living laboratory," where the art of conscious loving is a daily practice.

"We are really excited about what we're discovering in our own relationship," says Katie, "and what other people are discovering. It's not so much a recipe as it is a set of approaches that allow you to keep experiencing your relationship as a place of renewal and a place where there's freshness. So you get to go deep, but also have the experience of things being brand new all over again. It's never too late. With this focus on conscious loving at midlife and beyond—no matter what your relationship history has been—you can not only reinvent love, but you can invent love for yourself and you can reinvent your relationship."

Body Intelligence

At the heart of the Hendricks' work is the concept of body intelligence. People are familiar with the concept of body language, but most of us aren't fully conscious of exactly what our body language is revealing about us, or how it affects communication with a partner. That's where body intelligence comes in. "We bring in what people are doing as well as what they are saying," Katie shares. "It's a completely expanded approach to relationships. It's not just talking about it; it's what's going on in the person's body."

Learning to Love Yourself

We've all heard about the importance of self care, and some of us have even heard it said that we need to love ourselves before we can truly love someone else. But what's the reality behind those words? Why does it really matter? "Underneath a lot of relationship problems," says Gay, "is one person who is feeling bad about themselves and they take it out on the relationship." Gay and Katie help people to recognize this unhealthy pattern and provide a clear path for healing.

Breaking Away from the Blame Game

One of the most destructive forces in a relationship is the tendency to blame the other person. When we blame others in an effort to protect ourselves, we end up hurting our partnership. "Blame is the crack cocaine of relationships," says Gay, "because it just takes a second to trigger a person's adrenaline and defensiveness. We have an antidote to that. You're always only ten seconds away from a breakthrough in relationships, but almost nobody knows that."

Great Sex in Midlife and Beyond

As a culture, we are programmed to believe that it's normal for sex after midlife to be anywhere from scarce to nonexistent. Gay and Katie share that this simply does not need to be true. "Relationships can be even better in the second half of life than they are in the first half of life," says Gay. "Sex can be better in the second half of life." Wondering what you can do to have your sexual relationships keep getting better after the age of 50? Gay and Katie cover the topic in detail in their new book, "Conscious Loving Ever After."

Read Gay and Katie's articles at www.HuffingtonPost.com/Kathlyn-and-Gay-Hendricks

For more information, visit www.Hendricks.com

Welcome to the online press kit for Allison Maslan

Serial entrepreneur and business mentor Allison Maslan shows people how to grow rock-star companies while living meaningful lives

Profit with Purpose

Everyone wants their business to succeed, but as we look around at the businesses we encounter every day in our communities, it is plain to see that some simply don't make it very far from their launching pads. So, what is the difference between a business that succeeds and one that doesn't? Why do some business owners struggle while others thrive? Serial entrepreneur and business mentor Allison Maslan has identified the "secret sauce" of business success and she shares it with her clients through her Pinnacle Global Business Coaching and Mastermind Program.

A Mentor Who Has Been There

These days, everyone is a life coach or business coach, from young adults fresh out of college to your next-door neighbor. In a world where it's hard to find a business coach that actually has the experience to support you, Allison Maslan stands apart as a true business mentor, business expert and empowerment leader. She has successfully built 10 companies in all different industries, including serving as a holistic physician for 20 years. Allison knows what it takes to build and grow a business, and she knows how to take business owners from surviving to thriving in their companies and their lives.

"You have so many Internet marketers out there saying, 'Make a million dollars,' and that's great," Allison says. "I'm all about having a profitable business. It's crucial… but you have to have a deeper meaning fueling you, giving you the energy to put the effort in that you need to succeed. When people don't succeed, it's not necessarily because they don't have the right strategy; it's because of their mindset. It's how they see the world and how they value their own self-worth."

Achieving Success, Living Your Life

The collegiate system in the Unites States pumps out graduate after graduate, many of whom end up feeling disillusioned by the sheer amount of money they spent on their education versus the reality of not being able to find a good job afterwards. The problem, according to Allison Maslan, is that "they don't necessarily know what it takes to be successful. They may not be willing to put in the energy, the commitment, the sweat to make themselves a success. They are seeing people out there making millions and even billions, and that is truly possible, but you have to have that secret sauce, a combination of drive, passion and strategy, to make it happen."

"We have more entrepreneurs coming into the marketplace than ever, including more women entrepreneurs than ever, but there are just certain proven qualities that it's going to take for people to succeed."

And it's not all about what Allison calls the "ninja-like focus" that successful entrepreneurs need to succeed; it's also about creating healthy outlets and a commitment to one's personal well-being. "Business owners are their own body's worst enemy," says Allison. "They are so driven to succeed, but they don't take care of themselves, so they can't succeed. You've got to make time for fun and relationships in your life. You've got to have a place where you can disconnect and not think about all your responsibilities and just be present."

Besides being a business mogul, Allison has been a trapeze artist for 17 years. "When I'm up there, I'm not thinking about any responsibilities. It is a great way to release stress and get refocused. I have to focus or I could get hurt. It's also about facing my fears. I face my fears every time I climb that ladder. I become more and more resilient, and in doing so up there, I become more and more resilient down here. The bigger the risk I take on the trapeze, the less that business or life challenges hold me back me on the ground."

Learn more at www.MyBlastOff.com

Welcome to the online press kit for Dr. Bradley Nelson

Dr. Bradley Nelson Heals Patients Through "Emotional Surgery"

The Emotion Code: Future Medicine Now

Modern science increasingly verifies a truth that runs through ancient healing systems: The mind and body are inextricably connected, with our thoughts and emotions exerting a powerful influence on our health. Probing the frontiers of our ability to heal physical and mental disease through "emotional surgery," Dr. Bradley Nelson is one of the world's foremost experts in the emerging fields of bio-energetic medicine and energy psychology.

From his more than 20 years practice as a holistic physician, Dr. Brad discerned that the vast majority of physical pain, disease and mental and emotional problems his patients suffered was rooted in trapped emotions, the unseen emotional baggage we all carry from hurtful life experiences.

"After twenty-some years and thousands of patients, I'm convinced that trapped emotions are at the basis of almost everything from phobias and anxiety attacks to cancers and fibromyalgia. The good news is that by clearing these trapped emotions, the symptoms of the disease or condition become noticeably better—and often the disease or condition itself completely disappears."

Through his studies of ancient medical practice and modern quantum physics, he developed The Emotion Code, a simple yet powerfully effective method anyone can learn to release the trapped emotions that block mental and physical healing.

The idea of energy medicine is certainly not new. Ancient records describe the use of energy for healing as far back 4000 BC. "The ancient Indian physicians who practiced Ayurvedic medicine called energy prana.

In traditional Chinese medicine, it is call qi or chi. Both of these systems, as well as 95 other ancient cultures, worked with energy in specific ways over the centuries to effect healing. But it's only with the advent of quantum physics that energy has really been acknowledged in contemporary western medicine."

Today we know that everything is made up of energy, from our bodies to the thoughts we think.

"Our bodies are really a collection of vast numbers of very small bits of energy that are flying in close formation," Dr. Brad explains.

Through his practice and studies, Dr. Brad realized that these bits of energy that make up our bodies are directly affected by the energy of our emotions. He also discovered that the energy of negative emotions can become trapped within the body, almost like a tumor, with potentially disastrous consequences to our physical and psychological well-being. He developed The Emotion Code to release these trapped emotions from the body.

"I start by accessing the intelligence of the subconscious mind, which is an incredible holographic computer that archives every moment of your day, everything you've ever eaten or tasted, or touched or smelled, the entire history of your health," he says.

After identifying a specific trapped emotion, simply passing any magnet (or even your own fingertips) along the Governing Meridian releases the energy of the trapped emotion. Dr. Brad's patients experience results that are nothing short of miraculous in everything from chronic fatigue to depression to back and shoulder pain.

Using his expertise as a computer programmer, Dr. Brad codified his techniques and created a "mind mapping" system that made his work highly reliable and repeatable.

"I have always been driven to empower people to help themselves, and I began teaching seminars to do just that in 1998," he says. "I have been all over the world teaching The Emotion Code, and it is spreading like wildfire now, all over the globe."

Today Dr. Brad is spreading the knowledge of The Emotion Code (as well as the advanced version, The Body Code System) internationally through his lectures and his best-selling book, The Emotion Code.

"We've taken energy healing and made it so powerful, and so simple and easy that even a child can do it. With the Emotion Code, people learn that they have access to a universal database of intelligence that they can easily and instantly access to promote their own healing."

Visit Dr. Bradley Nelson's public websites at www.DrBradleyNelson.com and www.TheEmotionCode.com

Bio Examples

About Allison Maslan

Byline BIO: Allison Maslan is a serial entrepreneur, having created and successfully run 10 different companies including cultivating a 20-year practice as a holistic physician. Her company Allison Maslan International offers Pinnacle Global, a three-tier business coaching program that teaches entrepreneurs how to accelerate their growth, capitalize on their success and balance it all with a meaningful life. Learn more about Allison and the Pinnacle Global programs at www.MyBlastOff.com

Broadcast BIO: Serial entrepreneur and business mentor Allison Maslan has created and successfully run 10 different businesses and she faces her fears on the trapeze. Allison, what is it that so many of today's entrepreneurs are missing when it comes to achieving success in life and work?

Full BIO: Allison Maslan is a serial entrepreneur, having created and successfully run 10 different companies including cultivating a 20-year practice as a holistic physician. She was named one of the Top Women Entrepreneurs Who Inspire by "Self Made Magazine." Her company Allison Maslan International offers Pinnacle Global, a three-tier business coaching program that teaches entrepreneurs how to accelerate their growth, capitalize on their success and balance it all with a meaningful life. As a trapeze artist, Allison shares her unique experience of facing fears to achieve results. She is the author of the Amazon #1 bestseller "Blast Off!: The Surefire Success Plan to Launch Your Dreams into Reality," and was recently featured in the documentary film "Inspired by Eleven," which follows the journey of 11 entrepreneurs. Learn more about Allison and the Pinnacle Global programs at www.MyBlastOff.com

About Roger W. Washington, M.D.

Byline BIO: A Stanford Medical School graduate and Academy of Family Physicians Fellow, Roger W. Washington, M.D. has answered the question, *"Doctor, Why Am I Sick?"* for 30 years. In his first book, "Lack of Sufficient SLEEP MATTERS," Dr. Washington decodes the root cause of illness he discovered in California's Silicon Valley, where sacrificing sleep is the norm. Learn more at www.SleepMattersTheBook.com

Broadcast BIO: Everyone who gets sick wants to know why and what they can do to prevent it from happening again. Our guest today is a medical doctor who has spent 30 years decoding the connection between stress, lack of sufficient sleep, and the cause of illness. Dr. Roger W. Washington is author of the new book "Lack of Sufficient SLEEP MATTERS" (visit www.SleepMattersTheBook.com). Welcome, Dr. Washington. How does lack of sufficient sleep contribute to illness?

Full BIO: A Stanford Medical School graduate and Academy of Family Physicians Fellow, Roger W. Washington, M.D. has answered the question, *"Doctor, Why Am I Sick?"* for 30 years. In his first book, "Lack of Sufficient SLEEP MATTERS," Dr. Washington decodes the root cause of illness he discovered in California's Silicon Valley, where sacrificing sleep is the norm. Son of a nurse and hospital attendant, and a father to teenagers Jared and Maya, Dr. Washington chose the all-encompassing medical training of a family practitioner to become a more effective healer as well as to realize his passion for teaching the principles of illness prevention.

Dr. Washington's start in life was very challenging. At the tender age of 2, he was separated from his single working mother Mary and placed in a Catholic orphanage. Three years went by before his father Bill and stepmother, the saintly Cornelia Farmer, found him and brought him to their loving home with his sister and brother. Growing up in and around low-income projects in Elizabeth and Newark, New Jersey, his love of learning and rabble-rousing brought him notoriety and good fortune. After staging school walkouts in protest of budget cuts and organizing an after-school African-American club, he received a leadership scholarship to attend Pingry, a prestigious country day high school. Later, he received academic scholarships for the underprivileged to attend Denison University in Ohio, Pomona College in Southern California, and Stanford in Northern California. It was at Stanford that he chose to become a family practitioner, rather than specialize as his peers were encouraged to do. He reasoned this would enable him to give back by building a practice where he could also administer to the underserved. Yes, even wealthy Silicon Valley has pockets of underserved populations.

Dr. Washington now sees his choice as being fortuitous because by going against the grain, once again, and seeking broad medical training in family practice he discovered his ability to deeply listen and respond to causations, not just symptoms and disease states. Over the course of 30 years of practice, his holistic perspectives of our role in illness, and his principles of illness prevention organically emerged. Eventually, he derived a theory that decodes the root cause of most disease in our *can-do* society.

In "Lack of Sufficient SLEEP MATTERS," Dr. Washington takes us into his practice with patient stories showing how he listens with great curiosity about their activities, states of mind, and emotions leading up to when they became ill. He shows us how a *crash and burn* pattern develops and then startles us with the common threads he found across all sorts of illnesses. When he traces these illnesses back to his patients' own habit patterns of dealing with life's pressures by *borrowing energy* to *accelerate* their day-time activities, we're floored to find an unpaid *sleep debt* at the nexus of them all. Not to leave the reader out of the equation, Dr. Washington derives *SICK Qs*, questions we all can ask ourselves, so we can decode the root cause of our own illness cycle.

As an idealist medical student who accepted scholarships for the disadvantaged, Dr. Washington made a commitment to making a difference in the world by teaching the principles of illness prevention. Little did he know it would lead to a theory that decodes the root cause of most disease—the lack of sufficient sleep.

In addition to his book, Dr. Washington's new non-profit organization, the Sleep to Live Well Foundation, plans classes and workshops to disrupt sleep-debt patterns that cause illness. He is also expanding his family practice to offer sleep therapy and coaching sessions for the more extreme cases. In his next book, The Euphoria of SLEEPING SOUNDLY, Dr. Washington will examine the power and gift of sleep, just how far out of touch our society is with sleep's true nature and purpose, and he'll rectify this by naturally realigning us with perception-altering insights and habit-changing coaching. Learn more at www.SleepMattersTheBook.com

About Dr. Bradley Nelson

Byline BIO: Author and international lecturer in bio-energetic medicine and energy psychology, Dr. Brad has successfully used The Emotion Code with thousands of patients around the globe to relieve symptoms and often effect cures in conditions ranging from depression to cancer. His best-selling book, The Emotion Code, offers step-by-step instructions for working with the body's own healing power. Learn more at www.DrBradleyNelson.com and www.TheEmotionCode.com

Broadcast BIO: Have you ever thought about how much your emotions influence your health? Our guest today, Dr. Bradley Nelson ("Dr. Brad") is one of the world's foremost experts in the emerging fields of bio-energetic medicine and energy psychology. Through his twenty-plus years as a holistic physician, he developed The Emotion Code, a system for releasing the trapped emotions that block mental and physical healing. Learn more at TheEmotionCode.com. Welcome, Dr. Brad. Why do you say emotions are the underlying cause of most physical and psychological disease?

Full BIO: Dr. Brad was raised in rural Montana and practically grew up on the back of a horse. As a child, Dr. Brad suffered two life-threatening illnesses – both of which were healed, not by traditional western medicine, but by separate alternative methods that tapped the power of energy. These experiences were to shape Dr. Brad's life going forward.

In college, Dr. Brad studied computer programming and decided to pursue a career in business. But just six months before entering the MBA program at Brigham Young University, he had an epiphany. "I had asked God for guidance about my future. One night, I woke up and my mind was overflowing with thoughts of service to mankind and to humanity. The feelings were absolutely overwhelming, and as my head was filled with thoughts of healing and helping the world, a voice that was crystal clear spoke to me saying, 'This is a sacred calling.'"

In response to this calling, Dr. Brad entered Life Chiropractic College West, in San Lorenzo, California in 1988. After graduating with honors, he began his practice as a holistic chiropractic physician and saw a wide variety of patients, many of whom had seemingly incurable conditions. "I remember my instructors saying that the brain is the most sophisticated computer in the known universe. And I thought, 'Wow. If the brain is really this super computer, how amazing it would be to access the data that is stored there to unlock keys to help these people heal.'"

Through extensive study in disciplines such as ancient medical practices, psychology and quantum physics as well as the guidance of his own spiritual practice, Dr. Brad discovered that packets of unprocessed emotion were the basis of most conditions. "The body is essentially energy, and emotion is energy as well. When the energy of a negative emotion is trapped in the body, it impacts the body's self-healing system. These trapped emotions are almost like tumors. At the least, they can obstruct healing. At their worst, they actually create disease and physical problems."

Using this knowledge, Dr. Brad designed processes that have created amazing results with complex problems like fibromyalgia, chronic fatigue syndrome, lupus, and even cancer. "I developed a method of accessing the intrinsic genius of my patients' subconscious minds. Once the trapped emotion is identified by the subconscious, we use the laws of energy and electro-magnetic fields and employ the Governing Meridian to release them. Though the process is based on some pretty sophisticated and subtle knowledge, we've made it so simple that even a child can do it." He calls the process The Emotion Code.

Based on his phenomenal success, Dr. Brad attracted patients from all over the country and Canada. "Somewhere along the line I developed a very powerful feeling that people could do a lot to help themselves. I had a deep, driving urge to empower people. So I began teaching seminars to do just that in 1998."

Dr. Brad continued his private practice and his teaching until 2004, when he realized that his method was destined for a broader audience. Selling his practice, Dr. Brad devoted his time to writing The Emotion Code which was published in 2007. "The success of that book has been astonishing to me. It taught me how powerful the written word is. There are people now on every continent and in nearly every country who are using The Emotion Code to get rid of their own emotional baggage and the best part is that they are helping their loved ones to do the same."

Today, as one of the world's foremost experts in the emerging fields of bio-energetic medicine and energy psychology, Dr. Brad spends his time lecturing internationally, writing articles, and developing the next iteration of The Emotion Code (The Body Code) and credential programs for The Emotion Code and The Body Code practitioners.

Father to seven children, Dr. Brad lives in St. George, Utah with his wife Jean and their two youngest children.

"I feel this is my calling: to help people use their own intrinsic genius to find trapped emotions and release them so that their pain goes away, their diseases improve and sometimes disappear, and they no longer have depression, anxiety, panic attacks, or phobias. They stop sabotaging themselves, improve their health, and often improve their love life by getting rid of their emotional baggage through The Emotion Code."

Learn more at www.DrBradleyNelson.com and www.TheEmotionCode.com

News and Story Ideas Examples

Allison Maslan

You've Launched Your Business. Now What?

You came up with a great business plan. You put in the legwork to take your plan from pipe dream to practical. You've had your launch date and you're open for business! Why aren't things running as smoothly as you imagined? Business mentor Allison Maslan helps entrepreneurs understand what it takes to succeed.

Not My Business? Perfect.

According to a recent Harvard study, some of the greatest business innovations and ideas may come from brainstorming with people outside of your industry. Business mentor and serial entrepreneur Allison Maslan provides this much-needed fresh perspective to business owners who are aiming to take their company to the next level of success.

Profit with Purpose

Having a highly profitable business is crucial, but if your work is just a job and not your passion, it will likely be fraught with struggle. Business mentor and serial entrepreneur Allison Maslan works with CEOs that want to fast track their success while creating a much more meaningful life.

How to Help Your Dream Business Succeed

You spent hours upon hours, year after year learning your particular craft or skillset. It was your dream to start your own company and make your passion your profession…but what do you do when you are a master at your craft but you don't know how to run a business? Allison Maslan explains the pitfalls of running a business without the proper support and structure.

Diagnosing Your Blocks to Success

Serial entrepreneur and business mentor Allison Maslan has successfully created and run 10 different companies, including her 20-year practice as a Certified Homeopathic Practitioner. She draws upon her experience to help entrepreneurs get to the root of their business problems, using a holistic approach that examines physical, mental and emotional roadblocks within the CEO and the organization.

A Business Plan for Your Love Life

For all those businesspeople out there who are great at their business but not at their love life, serial entrepreneur and business mentor Allison Maslan offers up her plan for using your business sense to invite the right kind of relationship into your life.

The Extreme Sport of Entrepreneurship

Launching and running your own business is like an extreme sport. You face your fears. You have to have determination, commitment and dedication. You have to show up even when you don't feel like it, even when you're in pain or tired. Trapeze artist, serial entrepreneur and business mentor Allison Maslan shares her story.

What They Didn't Teach You In College

So many of today's graduates are leaving school with a mountain of debt only to find that they can't get a job and don't know what to do next to succeed. Business mentor Allison Maslan successfully created and ran 10 different companies. Now, she is showing new grads how to do what it takes to find success.

Making Our Mark: Women In Business

Serial entrepreneur and business mentor Allison Maslan successfully created and ran 10 different companies, starting when she was a single mother. She says women are finally making their mark on the business world, but that there is still a long way to go.

What It Means to Be a Leader

What makes a successful leader and successful business? Why do some leaders succeed while others fail? Serial entrepreneur and business mentor Allison Maslan explains.

How to Develop a Hot Company Culture

Culture development within your business encourages the right kind of employees to flock to your company and improves employee retention. Serial entrepreneur and business mentor Allison Maslan explains how to make your company an attractive place to work and grow.

An Entrepreneur's Journey: How One's Dream Must Involve a Team

How to shift from being the one that jumped into business with a dream, to building a team that can get behind your vision. An astronaut set foot on the moon, but it was the team that sent him there.

Roger W. Washington, M.D.

Decoding the Root Cause of Illness
In his book, "Lack of Sufficient SLEEP MATTERS," Dr. Roger W. Washington explores the role of insufficient sleep as a root cause of a wide variety of illness. Dr. Washington explains how he determined that lack of sufficient sleep may be the single most common cause of people getting sick.

Restoring Balance to Life
By restoring our natural relationship to sleep, we can prevent Illness. It starts with understanding our role in this root cause of illness. Dr. Washington discusses how we can regain power over our own health, wellbeing and ability to prevent illness.

A.C.C.E.L.E.R.A.T.E.D.: High Risk Traits of Alpha Males and Females
Are you active, confident, creative and clever; do you feel like you sometimes have extra energy, or like you can get by with less sleep? Are you entrepreneurial, risk-taking, articulate, "Titanic" (feel able to carry on despite hardship), enthusiastic/empathetic and determined? Dr. Washington explains how these characteristics can indicate risks for illness and early death, with examples from his Silicon Valley practice.

Stop Compromising Your Health
Dr. Washington explains the science behind why lack of sufficient sleep harms the immune system and makes us vulnerable to a wide range of illnesses and diseases, including migraines, IBS, cancer, and even early death.

CRASHED: What Goes Up Must Come Down
Do you experience phases where you feel cranky, irritable, angry and anxious? Dr. Washington explains why we sometimes feel low-energy, lethargic and negative, especially after periods of exuberant activity and inadequate sleep.

The Washington Lack of Sufficient Sleep™ Principle
Based on 30 years of patient care and research, Dr. Washington derived a theory of illness, IaA/S, which states that our potential for Illness is proportional to Activity and inversely proportional to Sleep. He also discovered that illness usually strikes when activity slows down. He explains how engineers in Silicon Valley inspired these theories.

Am I Getting Enough Sleep?
Dr. Washington shares tips from his Washington LOSS™ principles and formula to help people determine if they are getting adequate amounts of rejuvenating sleep.

Night Owls, Delayed Sleep Phase Insomnia and the "Second Wind"
Some people do their best work at night. Others wake early and have trouble falling asleep, or find they are most creative and task-driven when they get a "second wind." Dr. Washington discusses how these patterns of having their "me-time" lead to disease.

Are You an Energy Borrower?

Dr. Washington explains how people unknowingly initiate the cycle of illness when they accelerate activities without rejuvenating their energy through proper sleep.

Relieving Symptoms of PMS

Dr. Washington has found that women who don't "energy borrow" from their sleep don't suffer from PMS. He explains how he has helped patients experience fewer symptoms of PMS and PMDD.

The "Sleep Whisperer"

Through his nonprofit organization, Live to Sleep Well Foundation, Dr. Washington is teaching people how to have a better relationship with sleep to become masters of our own health, wellness and even euphoria. He shares the foundation's work.

"Chronic" Illness: The Hidden Culprit

People suffering from chronic illness often have problems sleeping but they may not know that lack of sleep can be a root cause. Dr. Washington shares case studies of how Sleep LOSS™ has precipitated flares of chronic illness.

Retirement Age, Longevity and "Blue Death"

Do some firefighters and law officers really tend to die soon after retiring from high stress careers? Is there a connection between retirement age and longevity? Dr. Washington delves into the science behind these questions.

Igniting a Sleep Revolution

Is it really possible to get enough sleep in our hyper-connected, driven society? The answer is yes, once we understand the critical role sleep plays in our health. Dr. Washington discusses how he is spreading the word to help do this.

Maverick for Health

Early in his career Dr. Washington decided to buck the trend of doctors going into medicine with an eye on the money, opting instead for putting himself in a constant stream of fresh insights on health and wellness that comes with a family practice. He shares how he became passionately convinced that quality sleep is the root cause of illness so often overlooked by mainstream medicine.

Dr. Bradley Nelson

The Hidden Epidemic
Among thousands of patients he has treated, Dr. Brad estimates more than 90 percent suffer health effects related to past emotional trauma. He shares tools and techniques for uncovering and relieving the emotional roots of common illnesses, from depression and obesity to neck and back pain.

Alternative Medicine Breakthroughs
Dr. Brad demonstrates in live broadcasts how people can get instant, dramatic relief by uncovering emotional causes of pain and disease.

The Six Underlying Causes of Disease
From his more than 20 years practice as a holistic physician, Dr. Brad reveals hidden causes of emotional and physical pain and surprising new (and ancient) tools and techniques for healing.

Healing Depression, Anxiety & Loneliness
So many people suffer from, and are prescribed medications for, conditions that are rooted in past traumatic events. Dr. Brad tells how he helps patients uncover and overcome the root cause of their mental anguish.

When the Heart Won't Heal
Dr. Brad explains the latest research findings that confirm that the heart is more than a muscle or pump but the center of our emotional being. He shares case studies of how "heartbreak" can have traumatic effects for people in their health, careers and relationships, and reveals the keys to healing a broken heart.

Stress-Proof Your Health
The links between psychological stress and physical illness are well proven, from hypertension to depressed immune function. Dr. Brad explains and demonstrates proven techniques for relieving stress and bolstering energy and health.

Overweight? Emotional Causes and Cures
Dr. Brad explains the emotional triggers behind overeating, the invisible link between sadness and obesity and the five secrets people need to know to lose stubborn fat and get healthy.

Future Medicine for Healing Past Trauma
Just about everyone has suffered from emotional trauma, from bad breakups to hurts and crises in childhood and adolescence. When emotions are buried, they often resurface in the form of depression, anxiety or physical pain. Dr. Brad shares how he helps people uncover emotional wounds and find lasting healing.

Stop Blaming Mom or Dad

Mother's Day and Father's Day, family reunions and other holidays force us to confront relationships that may be far from ideal. Dr. Brad explains how people can heal themselves from emotional wounds of the past and improve their family relationships.

Healing the Incurable

Medical statistics are often discouraging on success rates for healing conditions like fibromyalgia, lupus, or severe depression. Dr. Brad shares inspirational success stories of patients who have returned to health from so-called incurable diseases.

Free to Love Again

People deeply wounded in love often experience an inability to trust, give and receive love and establish meaningful relationships, a condition Dr. Brad identifies as a "heart wall." He shares inspiring stories of patients who have lingering loneliness, isolation and sadness to find new love.

The Hendricks Institute

Does Your Partner Know Your Password?

Naturally, any healthy relationship must have trust at its core, but how does that translate into the digital age of cell phones, email, and social media? Is there such a thing as sharing too much? Relationship experts and bestselling authors of the new book, "Conscious Loving Ever After," tackle this modern love topic.

Body Language? Let's Talk Body Intelligence

Communication goes far beyond an exchange of words, and that's where body language comes in. According to relationship experts Gay and Katie Hendricks, however, it's important to take body language beyond the subliminal and into the realm of our conscious attention in order to achieve a level of awareness they call "body intelligence."

First, Love Yourself

We all know we should eat right, exercise, and do what it takes to keep a roof over our heads, but when it comes to the concept of truly loving ourselves, an astounding number of us are at a loss. Gay and Katie Hendricks, bestselling authors of the new book, "Conscious Loving Ever After," share why self-love is so important and how to begin the process of achieving it.

Midlife Relationship How-To

Everybody focuses on the birds and the bees, but what about the happily ever after? What does it mean to have a healthy, happy, exciting, and sexual relationship in midlife and beyond? Midlife relationships experts Gay and Katie Hendricks offer some tips from their new book, "Conscious Loving Ever After."

Blame: The Crack Cocaine of Relationships

Blame is one of the most toxic invaders into any relationship, triggering anger and defensiveness in mere seconds and sucking both people into a cycle of hurt. Relationship experts Gay and Katie Hendricks talk about why blame is so harmful and how to break painful patterns.

What Can Your Pets Tell You About Your Relationship?

People's pets reveal more about them than they may realize, from emotional tendencies to how they relate to the people closest to them. Relationship experts Gay and Katie Hendricks offer a closer look at what your pets say about your partnership.

Love in Later Life: It's Never Too Late

Bestselling authors and midlife relationship experts Gay and Katie Hendricks have been married for 34 years and say that the best relationships are possible in the second half of life—including the best sex! Find out how they do it and get tips from their new book, "Conscious Loving Ever After."

Money, Sex and Communication

The two biggest relationship struggles—and the causes of many an argument—are money and sex. Why do we get so triggered, and how can we avoid old, unhealthy patterns and embrace our best love yet? Relationship experts Gay and Katie Hendricks explain.

Interview Question Examples

Allison Maslan

1. In your book "Blast Off!" you taught people how to launch a successful business. Now, your Pinnacle Global program is showing entrepreneurs how to take their businesses to the next level. What are some of the most common pitfalls that entrepreneurs run into that can keep them from achieving their highest rate of success?

2. So many business owners are focused entirely on their bottom line. You talk about encouraging entrepreneurs to get away from the "dollars-per-hour model" so that they have room to create their success. How does that work?

3. People hear a lot about coaches…life coaches, business coaches. How is what you are doing different from what's out there?

4. You have said that your business is your life and that there's not really as simple of a separation as people would like to think. Why is it important for people to embrace their business as an integral part of their life?

5. You talk about the importance of having some sort of "time out" in life where you can set down all your responsibilities, such as what you do as a trapeze artist. How do these outlets contribute to a more healthy work life and business?

6. You were a homeopathic physician for 20 years. How does that inform the work you do now in helping entrepreneurs to diagnose the issues that are working against their success?

7. You've said that you met your soul mate later in life when you finally had a revelation about using your business sense to find the right partner. How did that work?

8. With so many young adults graduating into a job market that doesn't have anything to offer them, what can they do differently to achieve financial stability and success?

9. There are more women entrepreneurs today than ever. As you help entrepreneurs work around obstacles to achieve their highest rates of success, do find that female business owners face any unique challenges?

10. What is it that makes a company great to work for? How can business owners attract and retain employees?

Roger W. Washington, M.D.

1. You practice family medicine in Silicon Valley where the tech industry culture encourages innovation and entrepreneurial spirit over sleeping. What did these engineers have in common that led them to get sick?

2. In your book "Lack of Sufficient SLEEP MATTERS," you illustrate how people "borrow" energy by shortchanging themselves when it comes to rejuvenating sleep. How did you conclude this is the single most common cause of people getting sick?

3. You identified some high-risk traits of hard charging, successful people that lead to illness that you identify by the acronym A.C.C.E.L.E.R.A.T.E.D. What are these?

4. What is the "crashed and burned" syndrome you speak of in your book, and how does it explain why we often fall ill after going through stressful situations?

5. How can people change their overachieving, driven, workaholic lifestyles to stop compromising their health?

6. You say sleep can restore our natural and "normal" state of euphoria. What does this mean and what steps should people take?

7. What are some of the most common illnesses and diseases caused by lack of sufficient sleep?

8. What are some surprising ones that people would not think are related to sleep problems, but are?

9. What is the relationship between lack of sufficient sleep and PMS?

10. What is your Washington Lack of Sufficient Sleep™ (LOSS) Principle?

11. How can people determine if they are getting adequate amounts of rejuvenating sleep?

12. What are some steps people can take to improve their sleep?

13. In your book you discuss why some people do their best work late at night. Why is this?

14. What is the "second wind" and what does it have to do with getting quality sleep?

15. Many people have "delayed phase sleep insomnia" – they have difficulty falling asleep because of life's stresses. Some even awake in the middle of the night with stress and can't get back to sleep. How can people break out of this distressful sleep pattern?

16. How can a person tell if they are an "energy borrower?"

17. What is "Blue Death?" Why do some people die prematurely after retiring from high-stress careers?

18. What are some "chronic" illnesses that can be relieved through better sleep?

19. You had a very challenging early life, including being placed in an orphanage as a young child and growing up in and around low-income housing the projects in New Jersey. You ended up graduating from Stanford Medical School. How did your early life shape your career as a maverick who questioned conventional medicine?

20. You have started a nonprofit organization, Live to Sleep Well Foundation. What will it do and how do you plan to start a "sleep revolution?

Dr. Bradley Nelson

1. In treating thousands of patients over the years, you have come to believe that emotional trauma is the root cause of pain and disease in the vast majority of cases. How do you determine if physical symptoms are related to emotional causes?

2. What are the most common illnesses associated with what you call "trapped emotions?"

3. The techniques you use have been called "emotional surgery." How do you help people uncover and overcome the root causes of pain and illness?

4. How can people experience dramatic and immediate relieve from symptoms that have haunted them for years?

5. So many people are prescribed medication for depression, anxiety and other forms of mental and psychological distress. Can they really find lasting healing free of drugs?

6. What are some of the new research findings about the role of the human heart in our emotional and physical health?

7. Heartbreak is such a common term, but it is also a real condition that can cause ongoing problems in a person's life. What are some of the long-lasting effects of a "broken heart?"

8. Can people heal themselves from heartbreak? If so, how?

9. People are so stressed out today and it is harming their health. How can people become more resilient to stress in their lives?

10. Most of us have heard the term "emotional" eating. What are the emotions that trigger overeating and weight-gain?

11. How do you help your patients who are struggling to lose weight and get healthier?

12. Just about everyone suffers from some emotional trauma in life, from bad breakups to hurts and crises in childhood and adolescent. How are some people able to move on, while others experience long-lasting symptoms related to emotional pain?

13. Many people trace their emotional baggage to their parents and issues they had growing up. How do you help them find freedom from the past and better relationships with their parents and siblings as adults?

14. You have had remarkable success treating many conditions that have stymied conventional medicine, such as fibromyalgia, chronic fatigue syndrome and severe depression. How have you helped patients return to health from so-called incurable diseases?

15. People deeply wounded in love often experience an inability to trust, give and receive love and establish meaningful relationships, yet you have seen some miracles in this regard. What is the key for hurting people to find new love?

30-Second Elevator Pitch Examples

Pitch 1

Pamela Yellen is a financial security expert and bestselling author teaching people how to literally *bank on themselves*. She investigated more than 450 savings and retirement planning strategies seeking an alternative to the risk and volatility of stocks and other investments. Her research led her to a time-tested, predictable method of growing and protecting wealth she calls Bank On Yourself (www.BankOnYourself.com) that is now used by more than half a million people.

Pitch 2

Stress Elimination expert Don Goewey is the author of the new book, Mystic Cool, already topping the charts. Goewey (Say Go EEE) believes, "Rewiring your brain can have you experience less stress and generate creative brilliance." He has worked for more than three decades helping people reach their potential, including war refugees, prisoners, patients with life-threatening illness, business leaders, and others in high-stress occupations. His new book, Mystic Cool, provides a proven approach to transcending stress and unlocking creative potential. To learn more, visit www.MysticCool.com.

Pitch 3

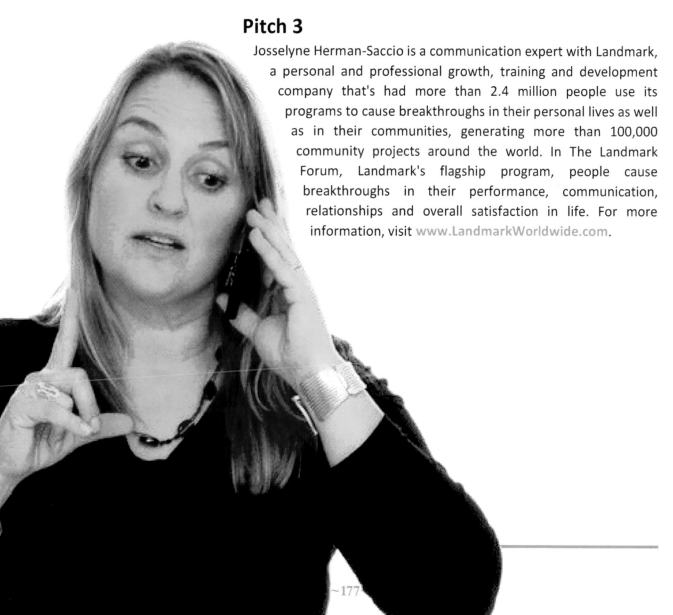

Josselyne Herman-Saccio is a communication expert with Landmark, a personal and professional growth, training and development company that's had more than 2.4 million people use its programs to cause breakthroughs in their personal lives as well as in their communities, generating more than 100,000 community projects around the world. In The Landmark Forum, Landmark's flagship program, people cause breakthroughs in their performance, communication, relationships and overall satisfaction in life. For more information, visit www.LandmarkWorldwide.com.

Email Pitch Examples

[Relationships] Body Language? Let's Talk Body Intelligence

Hello [FIRSTNAME]

Relationship experts and best-selling authors Gay and Katie Hendricks are helping thousands of couples across the world through both their new book, *Conscious Loving Ever After: How to Create Thriving Relationships at Midlife and Beyond,* and their transformational relationship seminars. One area that Gay and Katie teach couples to recognize and understand is what they call "body intelligence," a strong personal knowing that goes beyond body language.

Want to interview Gay and Katie? Contact me, and read on for more details.

Body Language? Let's Talk Body Intelligence

Communication goes far beyond an exchange of words, and that's where body language comes in. In fact, Stanford scientists recently discovered that body language can predict creative output or learning ability.

According to relationship experts Gay and Katie Hendricks, it's important to take body language beyond the subliminal and into the realm of our conscious attention in order to achieve a level of awareness they call "body intelligence."

"We bring in what people are doing as well as what people are saying," said Katie. "It's a completely expanded approach to relationships. It's not just talking about it; it's what's going on in the person's body."

To gain body intelligence:

1. **Observe what your body is doing both when speaking and listening.** Are your arms crossed? Are you facing your partner or turned away? Is your head up, down or at an angle?

2. **Receive the information your body is sending to you.** What does your body position or motion tell you about your feelings?

3.   **Try something new.** What happens if you move your body to a more receptive, open position?

Gay and Katie Hendricks guide couples in first becoming of aware of and experiencing body intelligence, and then using it to communicate more openly and honestly.

About: Relationship experts Gay and Kathlyn Hendricks have been married 35 years, worked together for 30 years and have authored over 30 books, including their bestselling *Conscious Loving* and their new book, *Conscious Loving Ever After*. They have offered seminars worldwide and appeared on more than 500 radio and television shows, including OPRAH, CNN, CNBC, 48 HOURS and others. They operate The Hendricks Institute in Ojai, Calif.

Online Press Kit: www.HendricksInstitute.OnlinePressKit247.com

Websites:
1.   www.Hendricks.com
2.   www.FoundationForConsciousLiving.com
3.   www.HeartsInTrueHarmony.com

For interviews, contact me and I will be happy to assist you.

@MichelleTennant
International Publicist, Chief Creative Officer
Wasabi Publicity, Inc.

[Back to School] 5 Ways to Teach Kids About Money

Hello [FIRSTNAME]

Kids are back in school comparing the clothes and things they have with those of their classmates and falling for the advertisers' line that have to spend lots of money to be happy. I have two-time New York Times Bestselling Author Pamela Yellen with **practical ways parents can teach their kids to spend and save responsibly** (the ones below are for middle schoolers and she also has great lessons for grade school and high school students.) Read on for details and contact me for interview requests.

5 Tips to Teach Kids to Spend and Save Wisely

Here are some of Pamela's tips for teaching kids money lessons that will help them through life:

1. **Discuss Commercials With Your Kids** – Sit down with your kids, and watch ads on TV. Ask them what the commercial is trying to sell them. Discuss the underlying messages, such as "All cool kids have this!" and "Other kids will like you if you have this!" And talk about how advertisers try to manipulate us. Have them compare how incredible a product looks in an ad with how it often looks in real life. A fast food burger is a great example!

2. **Teach Them the Difference Between Wants and Needs** – Give them examples, such as the difference between lunch money and money for comics, or clothes for school and a new bike. Guide them with questions, such as, "What's the worst that can happen if you don't get that comic? How about if you don't get lunch? Do you need that new iPod, or just want it?"

3. **Share Lessons While Shopping** – When you are at a store and they see something they want that's not on the day's shopping list, you don't have to have an argument, and you don't have to give in. Instead, simply say, "We'll have to go home and see if you have enough money in your spending (or savings) envelope to buy it." When they buy things, ask them how they feel about those purchases in the days after. Are they still excited about them? Any buyer's remorse? Is there anything they now feel might have been a better use for that money? Keep the pressure off, and let them know that purchasing mistakes are nothing more than great learning opportunities. Share your own lessons in this area.

4. **Teach Delayed Gratification** – Too often, kids are more than willing to settle for something of lower value now, rather than waiting for something of greater value later. Help your kids understand the benefits of delayed gratification by offering your child an option: "Would you rather I give you five dollars now, or do you want to wait two weeks, and I will give you 15 dollars

then?" If they're not sure you'd actually give them that 15 bucks in two weeks, let them watch you put 15 dollars in an envelope, seal it, and write their name on it, then put it in a safe place. Let them decide—five dollars now or 15 dollars in two weeks—and have them tell you why they chose that option. Discuss which option is a better alternative, and why. Then give them the opportunity to change their mind.

5. **Introduce Your Children to Comparison Shopping** – Help them develop comparison worksheets that show pros, cons, and the cost of a particular item. For example, if they're eager for a new bike, have them list potential candidates. Get on the Internet or go to the store, and research features of each one. Find a way to "test drive" those bikes. Look up consumer reviews.

"Get them fully involved in making well-considered spending decisions. Avoid the urge to do this work for them! In the end, they may not opt for the bike you would have chosen. But they'll learn so much more than they would by merely following your lead."

About the Author: Pamela Yellen is a financial investigator and the author of two New York Times best-selling books, including her latest, *The Bank on Yourself Revolution: Fire Your Banker, Bypass Wall Street, and Take Control of Your Own Financial Future*. Pamela investigated more than 450 financial strategies seeking an alternative to the risk and volatility of stocks and other investments, which led her to a time-tested, predictable method of growing wealth now used by more than 500,000 Americans.

Pamela can share additional money lessons for kids from young children to college age.

To learn more, visit her online press kit, www.PamelaYellen.OnlinePressKit247.com and the public site www.BankOnYourself.com. If you would like to interview Pamela, please contact me

Regards,

Jennifer Thomas, APR
PR Consultant
Wasabi Publicity, Inc.

BARNET**BAIN**

[Author Interview] Creativity Blocked? Try Picasso-ing!

Hello [FIRSTNAME]

Researchers at Rutgers University's Art and Artificial Intelligence Laboratory have come up with a "creativity algorithm" that explains why we love great works of art by masters such as Picasso. I have Academy Award-winning filmmaker and author Barnet Bain to share an exercise for how anyone can tap into their innate creativity to boost success in life and work. Read on for details and please contact me if you would like to speak with Barnet.

An Exercise for Drawing Your Solutions

Producer of "What Dreams May Come," the Academy Award-winning film starring the late Robin Williams, and author of the new book, "The Book of Doing and Being: Rediscovering Creativity in Life, Love and Work," Barnet teaches creativity workshops and classes at Columbia University.

What made Picasso and other great artists so creative was they "found a way to express an idea that was bigger than the experience of the world, yet in a way that the world could experience it," Barnet says. He shares his own technique for boosting creativity and finding solutions to problems that he calls "Picasso-ing." Here's how it works:

Preparation: Select your art supplies. Find the paper you like. Choose the drawing tools that you enjoy— pens, colored pencils, pastels, crayons, markers, or a combination thereof.

STEP 1: Bring to mind a problem that you are having, whether big or small. Without getting mired in it, go ahead and see it, sense it, feel it.

STEP 2: With your paper and drawing tools, give yourself the freedom to address the problem with artful abandon. This drawing practice is most effective when you are doing it abstractly. In that way, you will be welcoming the unlimited resources of your imagination. In no particular order...

1.   Draw your problem.
2.   Draw your feelings.
3.   Draw your desires.
4.   Draw your solution(s).

STEP 3: Make a commitment to yourself to act on the solution (or solutions) you have drawn.

"When we draw, dance, run, make love, we are introducing underutilized body intelligences into our creative process," Barnet says. "By coming home to the body, we access creative awareness and embodied potentials that are beyond logic and reason."

About the Author: Barnet Bain is an award-winning filmmaker, radio broadcaster, educator and creativity expert, and author of "The Book of Doing and Being" (Atria, 2015). His film credits include Oscar-winner "What Dreams May Come" (producer), Emmy-Award nominee, Outstanding TV Movie, "Homeless to

Harvard" (executive producer) and "The Celestine Prophecy" (writer, producer). He is also director, co-executive producer and scriptwriter "Milton's Secret," a family drama coming in 2016 based on the book by acclaimed spiritual author Eckhart Tolle and Robert S. Friedman and starring Donald Sutherland.

Web: www.BarnetBain.com

Online Press Kit: www.BarnetBain.OnlinePressKit247.com

For interview requests, please contact me.

@MichelleTennant
Wasabi Publicity, Inc.

[Business] Bad Boss? Ask these 3 questions

Hello [FIRSTNAME]

Three out of every four employees report that their boss is the worst and most stressful part of their job, and 65 percent would rather have a new boss than a pay raise, according to a leading business magazine. Even more concerning, employees who have a "bad boss" have significantly higher rates of heart disease than those who don't. I have author and corporate leadership consultant Anne Grady with **three questions you can ask before communicating with your boss that can help improve difficult work relationships.** Contact me if you wish to interview Anne and read on for details.

Try This for Better Communication / Better Relationships:

In her 20 years of leadership development and communication consulting, Anne has worked with both staff and management and heard **how they often have different takes on the exact same issues.** This can make communication challenging and "if you're not able to communicate effectively, you are more likely to be unhappy at work," she says.

Here are three questions to ask before speaking with your boss that will help:

1. **Does it need to be said?** Is this issue important? If it is, communicate assertively and focus on being solution-oriented. If the issue isn't that important in the grand scheme of things, let it go.

2. **Does it need to be said by me?** Are you better off waiting for the message to come from someone else, or should it come from you? Your cranky co-worker has come in late for the fifth time this month. Is it really your responsibility to point it out? If it's directly impacting your work, it might be. But if it doesn't, let it go.

3. **Does it need to be said by me right now?** Timing is everything. Sometimes the exact same message may be received very differently depending on when it's delivered. Next time you're in a meeting and have the urge to disagree with your boss in front of the entire team, is it the right time to vocalize it? It might be worth the risk, depending on the issue. Or, it might make more sense to bring it up at a different time.

"While the questions are simple, it's actually quite difficult to catch yourself in the moment to ask them," Anne says. "Given that we spend the large majority of our waking hours at work, it stands to reason that anything you can do to make that experience easier is a no brainer. So before you say something you may regret, before you challenge the issue, voice your opinion, or put your foot in your mouth, take a moment to ask yourself these questions. Your manager will thank you, your relationship will improve, and you'll be happier at work."

About Anne: Anne Grady is an author, corporate leadership consultant and expert in personal and organizational transformation. With humor, passion and straight talk, she grew her business as a nationally recognized speaker and consultant while raising her severely mentally ill son. Anne shares lessons she has learned in her book, "52 Strategies for Life, Love and Work."

For more information, see www.AnneGradyGroup.com or visit Anne's online press kit, www.AnneGradyGroup.OnlinePressKit247.com.

To speak with Anne contact me.

Regards,

Jennifer Thomas, APR
PR Consultant
Wasabi Publicity, Inc.

[Health] Overweight? Emotional Causes and Cures

Hello [FIRSTNAME]

Need a holistic health expert to explain how people turn trauma into pounds, and how to stop this process and prevent it from occurring in the future? Dr. Bradley Nelson is one of the world's foremost experts in bio-energetic medicine and energy psychology. He details how people turn negative emotions into physical ailments like excessive weight gain and how to heal and regain our health. To interview Dr. Brad, contact me. @MichelleTennant

Overweight? Emotional Causes and Cures

Did you know that adult obesity rates (www.HealthyAmericans.org/Obesity) in America have doubled from 15% to 30% since 1980? Obesity is one of the leading causes of heart disease, depression and many other maladies. So, why are people packing on all this excess weight? According to Dr. Bradley Nelson, it is often due to negative emotions that get trapped within the body. Dr. Brad explains the invisible link between negative emotions and compromised health and shares the three secrets people need to know to lose stubborn fat and get healthy.

"Trapped emotions can cause you to...create depression, anxiety and other unwanted feelings that you can't seem to shake. They can interfere with proper function of your body's organs and tissues, wreaking havoc with your physical health." To stop weight gain in its tracks and begin healing:

1. **Find Your Triggers:** Notice when you feel most compelled to overeat. What are your emotions telling you about these times? Are you stressed? Worried? Sad?

2. **Start Journaling About Your Triggers:** Journaling allows you to shed light on the truth behind why you are overeating. Acknowledging your emotions and processing them will help to prevent them from getting trapped inside you and coming out in unhealthy ways.

3. **Use the Sway Test Around Food:** The Sway Test is a method of getting answers from your subconscious. Simply stand comfortably with your feet shoulder width apart, relax into that space and make an affirmative statement about eating the food in front of you. If your body wants it, you should shortly notice that you begin to sway gently forward. If your body rejects it, you should notice it swaying gently backwards.

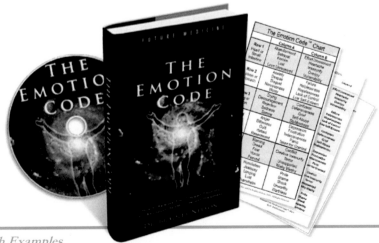

About Dr. Bradley Nelson: Author and international lecturer in bio-energetic medicine and energy psychology, Dr. Brad has successfully used The Emotion Code with thousands of patients around the globe to relieve symptoms and often affect cures in conditions ranging from depression to cancer. His best-selling book, *The Emotion Code*, offers step-by-step instructions for working with the body's own healing power.

WEB: www.DrBradleyNelson.com and www.TheEmotionCode.com

ONLINE PRESS KIT: www.DrBradleyNelson.OnlinePressKit247.com

For interviews, contact me.

@MichelleTennant
Wasabi Publicity, Inc.

About the Authors

L. Drew Gerber is CEO of Wasabi Publicity, Inc. With business partner Michelle Tennant Nicholson, Gerber co-created www.PitchRate.com, a free media tool that connects journalists and producers with the highest rated experts. Gerber's business practices and staffing innovations have been revered by *PR Week*, *Good Morning America*, and the *Christian Science Monitor*. His companies handle international PR campaigns and his staff develops online press kits for authors, speakers, and companies with Online PressKit 24/7 (www.OnlinePressKit247.com), a technology he developed for publicists.

20 Year PR Veteran and co-owner of Wasabi Publicity, **Michelle Tennant Nicholson** has seen PR transition from typewriters to Twitter. Called a five star publicist by *Good Morning America's* Mable Chan, Michelle specializes in international PR working regularly with the likes of *Oprah*, *Larry King*, the *BBC*, *The Today Show*, and all major media. Recently she secured *Dr. Phil* for a client only 8 hours after signing the contract. Follow her PR blog, www.StorytellerToTheMedia.com, where she teaches tips from the trade.

For more information, visit www.WasabiPublicity.com